UNDERSTANDING
RAYMOND CARVER

Understanding Contemporary American Literature

Matthew J. Bruccoli, *Editor*

UNDERSTANDING
Raymond
CARVER

by ARTHUR M. SALTZMAN

UNIVERSITY OF SOUTH CAROLINA PRESS

Published in Columbia, South Carolina, by the
University of South Carolina Press

Manufactured in the United States of America

Library of Congress Cataloging-in-Publication Data

Saltzman, Arthur M. (Arthur Michael), 1953–
    Understanding Raymond Carver / by Arthur M. Saltzman.
        p.   cm. — (Understanding contemporary American literature)
    Bibliography: p.
    Includes index.
    ISBN 0–87249–581–7. ISBN 0–87249–582–5 (pbk.)
    1. Carver, Raymond—Criticism and interpretation. I. Title.
II. Series
PS3553.A7894Z88 1988
813′.54—dc19   88–17237
                                                          CIP

Once again,
for Marla

CONTENTS

EDITOR'S PREFACE

Understanding Contemporary American Literature has been planned as a series of guides or companions for students as well as good nonacademic readers. The editor and publisher perceive a need for these volumes because much of the influential contemporary literature makes special demands. Uninitiated readers encounter difficulty in approaching works that depart from the traditional forms and techniques of prose and poetry. Literature relies on conventions, but the conventions keep evolving; new writers form their own conventions—which in time may become familiar. Put simply, *UCAL* provides instruction in how to read certain contemporary writers—identifying and explicating their material, themes, use of language, point of view, structures, symbolism, and responses to experience.

The word *understanding* in the series title was deliberately chosen. Many willing readers lack an adequate understanding of how contemporary literature works; that is, what the author is attempting to express and the means by which it is conveyed. Although the criticism and analysis in the series have been aimed at a level of general accessibility, these introductory volumes are meant to be applied in conjunction with the works they cover. Thus they do not provide a substitute for the works and authors they introduce, but rather prepare the reader for more profitable literary experiences.

M. J. B.

ACKNOWLEDGMENTS

Grateful acknowledgment is made to the following publishers for permission to reprint copyrighted material:

Will You Please Be Quiet, Please? McGraw-Hill Book Company. Copyright © 1976 by Raymond Carver.
Furious Seasons and Other Stories. Capra Press. Copyright © 1977 by Raymond Carver.
What We Talk About When We Talk About Love. Alfred A. Knopf, Inc., a division of Random House, Inc. Copyright © 1981 by Raymond Carver.
Fires: Essays, Poems, Stories. Capra Press. Copyright © 1983 by Raymond Carver.
Cathedral. Alfred A. Knopf, Inc., a division of Random House, Inc. Copyright © 1983 by Raymond Carver.
Where Water Comes Together with Other Water. Alfred A. Knopf, Inc., a division of Random House, Inc. Copyright © 1985 by Raymond Carver.
Ultramarine. Alfred A. Knopf, Inc., a division of Random House, Inc. Copyright © 1986 by Raymond Carver.

UNDERSTANDING
RAYMOND CARVER

Raymond Carver died August 2, 1988,
after a prolonged battle with lung cancer.

CHAPTER ONE

Connoisseur of the Commonplace

Career

Raymond Carver depicts the cramped conditions of working-class existence with genuine sympathy and authority. He was born in Clatskanie, Oregon, in 1938 and grew up in Yakima, Washington, where he hunted and fished and became an avid reader of Westerns and outdoor magazines. When he graduated from high school, he followed his father by working in the sawmill; by the age of twenty he was married and had two children, a situation he later described in "Fires" as one of "unrelieved responsibility and permanent distraction."

In 1958 Carver moved his debt-ridden family to California. He worked a series of low-paying jobs, including delivery man, gas station attendant, and hospital janitor, while his wife waited tables and sold door-to-door. Carver also enrolled part-time at Chico State College and came under the influence and encouragement of John Gardner, who was then an unpublished novelist. Carver transferred to Humboldt State College, where he earned his bachelor's degree in English in

1

1963. Then came a year at the prestigious Iowa Writers Workshop, followed by a trip to Israel occasioned by his wife's study-abroad scholarship. On leave from his first white-collar job editing for Science Research Associates (SRA), Carver had already published many of the poems that would go into *Near Klamath*, as well as some of the stories that would eventually appear in *Will You Please Be Quiet, Please?* and *Furious Seasons*. However, the trip was a major disappointment. Carver did no writing in Israel, and soon after their return home he began to drink heavily.

Carver was fired from SRA in 1970, but he won a National Endowment for the Arts Discovery Award for Poetry that freed him to write full time. Within the year he completed most of *Will You Please* and a second poetry collection, *Winter Insomnia*. Then in 1971 Gordon Lish, fiction editor for *Esquire*, published "Neighbors," and Carver had broken into the "slicks"—national periodicals with large readerships—in which he would soon become a fixture. He obtained several temporary university lectureships in creative writing, as well as the Joseph Henry Jackson Award for fiction. However, the rapid growth of his literary reputation, highlighted by three consecutive appearances in William Abraham's annual *Prize Stories: The O. Henry Awards* and a 1977 National Book Award nomination for *Will You Please*, contrasted sharply with his domestic problems (he and Maryann would divorce in 1982) and his alcoholic decline. On 2 June 1977 Carver stopped drinking for good.

CONNOISSEUR OF THE COMMONPLACE

The past ten years have provided abundant testimony to the recovery of the man and the continued development of the artist. Carver received a Guggenheim fellowship for 1977–78 and a second National Endowment of the Arts Award for fiction in 1979. The critical acclaim and popular success of both *What We Talk About When We Talk About Love* (1981) and *Cathedral* (1984), the latter earning National Book Critics Circle and Pulitzer Prize nominations, have vaulted Carver to the forefront of the contemporary literary scene and set the standard for the "new wave" of minimalist American writing. At present Carver lives with the poet Tess Gallagher. He is on the faculty of Syracuse University, and splits his time between New York and Port Angeles, Washington. In 1983 Carver received the prestigious Mildred and Harold Strauss Living Award from the American Academy and Institute of Arts and Letters. In a 1984 interview in the *New York Times Magazine*, he offered this assessment of his craft: "It's important to do the work because somebody needs to do it. It's important to be reminded that we're human. . . . I think it's a noble undertaking, this business."

Overview

Raymond Carver's characters work for a living. They fret about mortgages and dream about vacations. They watch television, talk on the telephone, live among brand names, wonder about their neighbors.

They know about pollution, laugh and cry at the movies, shake their heads at the news. They are bowlers, hunters, fishermen, cardplayers. Their families are dear to them, but there are inevitable misunderstandings, silences, infidelities—all the standard rifts and fractures love is prey to. Carver's characters smoke and drink more than they know they should. They complain about their misfortunes, harbor resentments, fear the future. Vaguely unhappy, vaguely lonesome, they tread water. They wonder if they are leading the right lives.

Carver's characters inhabit the world immediately recognizable as proletarian America, a terrain of fast food, used cars, and garish billboards. How so steadfastly pedestrian a literary environment as this has achieved so substantial an impact on contemporary American fiction is the chief motivation behind the critical fascination Raymond Carver has occasioned to date. He has been credited with the restoration of a presumably moribund form—literary realism. The well-wrought ambushes and exposures that constitute his celebrated collections of short stories have earned Carver the reputation of being among the leaders of a new movement in short fiction that is characterized by flatness of narrative tone, extreme spareness of story, an obsession with the drab and quotidian, a general avoidance of extensive rumination on the page, and, in sum, a striking restraint in prose style. This movement, whose most notable practitioners also include Ann Beattie, Elizabeth Tallent, Tobias Wolff, Mary Robison, and Frederick Barthelme, is typically referred to as

CONNOISSEUR OF THE COMMONPLACE

"minimalism," a designation that highlights the spartan technique and the focus on the tiny fault lines that threaten to open out into violence or defeat.

The controversy surrounding such fiction is apparent in the more disparaging headings it has garnered which brand it as formulaic and faddish: "K-Mart Realism," "Hick Chic," "Freeze-Dried Fiction," "TV Fiction," "Hi-Tech Fiction," "Postliterate Literature," "Lo-Cal Literature," "White Trash Fiction," "Postalcoholic Blue-Collar Minimalist Hyperrealism," "Around-the-house-and-in-the-yard Fiction," "Coke Fiction."[1] The thinly concealed indictment has less to do with the ordinariness of subject matter—the battle to establish literary attention for things so small was won generations ago—than with the possible failure of artistic nerve or the surrender to inhibition, as though what is really minimal about minimalism is the withered muse behind it or the decision to cater to the lowest common denominator of the contemporary reading public. Reviewers who praise Carver's refreshing readability and admire his expert delineation of the underside of the American Dream also seem eager to press Carver into service against postmodern elitists such as William Gaddis, Joseph McElroy, and Thomas Pynchon, who, so the argument usually concludes, pride themselves on creating texts so pure that few readers dare violate them. If minimalism is a reaction against postmodern pyrotechnics, what positive alternative direction for fiction does it present? Carver and company must stand trial for abdicating postmodern excesses only to succumb to an arid reserve—narrative voice shell-shocked by a hostile reality into a muddled monotone.

James Atlas, for example, claims that Carver's stories are severe to the point of anorexia. He laments a style that is "so aggressive in the suppression of detail, that one is left with a hunger for the richness, texture, excess, just as the cubed glass high-rises of Manhattan frustrate the eye's longing for nuance."[2] John Barth, himself a devout "maximalist" author, perhaps inadvertently furthers the suspicion of writers like Carver by noting that a central reason for their popularity is probably the decline in literacy and the diminishment of reading habits among the television generation, which is to say that the general reader cannot handle more than the minimalists require of him.[3] By extension there is the question of whether the obvious influence of minimalism upon the "M.F.A. Mafia," as Jerome Klinkowitz terms them, is really due to the sheer convenience of the "less is more" philosophy. If the glib aesthetic of the 1960s was that anything and anyone could be proclaimed a work of art, the "happening" fiction of the 1980s may mark a comparable trend.[4] Charles Newman goes so far as to diagnose the spread of minimalism to be part of "the classic conservative response to inflation—underutilization of capacity, reduction of inventory, and verbal joblessness," which simply rivets literary evolution to its inevitable socioeconomic context.[5] The "cultural weightlessness" of minimalism—its assumptions of sociopolitical impotence and enervated sensibilities—is, in Newman's estimation, a methodol-

CONNOISSEUR OF THE COMMONPLACE

ogy by which characters and authors alike are held captive: "Now it seems that the narrator is dragged down by his characters, adopting their limitations and defects, so that the reader is let off the hook by an author who refuses to attribute to him any curiosity—a strange deflection in which the reader does not blame the writer but rather feels superior to the characters."[6]

To counter these accusations effectively, we must begin by recognizing that while minimalist fiction obviously departs from the stylistic preening and playfulness of the works of Raymond Federman, Gilbert Sorrentino, and Ronald Sukenick, it does retain a concern with the intricacies of craft. Like Stanley Elkin and William Gass, for instance, Raymond Carver is a diligent refiner of sentences; the difference, however, is that whereas the former are masters of fusion and rhythmic embellishment, Carver is a surgeon who concentrates on taking sentences and "paring them down to where they seem solid somehow."[7] Much has been written about Carver's attempts to develop a style relevant to the plague of inarticulateness that his characters endure. Proceeding only so far as the vernacular will allow, experience is bounded by the impoverished vocabulary of consciousness. Dialogues are brief, hedged, and in the shadow of what they need to be about. Gass discovers in such radical divestment of development faddishness swollen to creed: "Images are out. It is fraudulent to poeticize. Kept simple, short, direct, like a punch, the sentences avoid subordination, qualification, subtlety. Subordination requires judgment, evaluation; it creates complexity, demands definition."[8] The numbing nature of contemporary life—postatomic and atomized, where communication dwindles as information proliferates—is inherent in the verbal incapacity that pervades these stories:

"I can't think of anything else. You go now. Tell me what you'd like."

"I don't know. Lots of things," he mumbled.

"Well, tell me. We're just talking, aren't we?"

"I wish you'd leave me alone, Nan."

—*"The Student's Wife"*

"What's wrong with here?" Jack said. "What would you guys do in Alaska? I'm serious. I'd like to know."

Carl put a potato chip in his mouth and sipped his cream soda. "I don't know. What did you say?"

After a while Jack said, "What's in Alaska?"

"I don't know," Carl said. "Ask Mary. Mary knows. Mary, what am I going to do up there?"

—*"What's in Alaska?"*

"What are you staring at me for?" he asks. "What is it?" he says and lays his fork down.

"Was I staring?" I say and shake my head stupidly, stupidly.

—*"So Much Water So Close to Home"*

"We're just talking. I just asked you how well you knew me. Would I"—how should he put it?—"am I trustworthy, for instance? Do you trust me?" It wasn't clear to him what he was asking, but he felt on the edge of something.

"Is it important?" she said. She looked at him steadily. . . .

CONNOISSEUR OF THE COMMONPLACE

He shrugged. "If you don't think it is, then I guess it isn't."

—*"The Pheasant"*

There were things he wanted to say, grieving things, consoling things, things like that.

—*"A Serious Talk"*

He said, "I just want to say one more thing."
But he could not think what it could possibly be.

—*"One More Thing"*

Crises arise in these stories when words are called to account for being inadequate to the task of conveying intentions.

The initial definition of minimalism as a kind of re-assumption of traditional realism succeeding the stylistic libertinism of postmodernism is a reaction to, and welcoming of, the comparative hospitality of minimalist fictions to the common reader. Whereas the occasional dour academic might feel his solitary way along the dark and airless corridors of William Gaddis or Thomas Pynchon, the public wants literature that opens windows onto the world they know. In keeping with this logic, the prodigality of postrealist or surfictionist splinter groups has lost its momentum, and, as confirmed by the healthy sales statistics mounted by the new breed of short story writers, fiction has begun to regain its sanity.

Closer to the mark, however, is a definition of minimalism that treats it as another postmodern tributary in the multifarious progress of American literary history.

Although their "experiments" with language are subtler than those of the more notorious desecrators of literary realism, the minimalists share their suspicion of the referential adequacy of words; at the same time, they share their clinical appreciation of the cadences of sentences. Raymond Carver, Ann Beattie, Mary Robison, Tobias Wolff, and writers like them are just as mannered and, in effect, just as subversive in their rigid jurisdiction over expansiveness as, at the other extreme, so-called maximalist writers like John Barth, T. Coraghessan Boyle, William Gaddis, William Gass, Joseph McElroy, Thomas Pynchon, and Ronald Sukenick are in their supermagnification and overregistration. It would be naïve, as well as inappropriate to the judiciously sucked-clean style of minimalism, to decide that it has miraculously come into being over the past decade or has that it has been so utterly innocent of the inroads and departures of postmodernism. (That so many minimalist authors teach or have taught in university classrooms further attests to the likelihood that they proceed in full awareness of their literary historical context.)

In short, if one of the main achievements of postmodern innovation in literature has been to broaden the scope of what and how a story can "be about," surely minimalism rates attention as a resulting option. As Kim A. Herzinger declares, minimalist writers "may well be creating literary constructs as formally rigorous and linguistically savvy as their postmodern predecessors. They are not, it seems to me, involved in a backbench effort to return to a pre-modern or pre-postmodern 'realism' " and could not achieve such a return even if they desired to, not after over half a century's worth of distrust of the representative powers of their medium. "Where the traditional 'realists' had a world and used a complex of ideas and emotions—done up in language—to describe it, the 'minimalists' have a complex of ideas and emotions—done up in language—which they use the world to describe."[9] As a radical divestiture of the sheer density to which realism conventionally ascribes—think of the weighty Henry James, William Dean Howells, or Theodore Dreiser, whose assiduous descriptions bespeak confident, noble enterprise—minimalism represents a challenge to the authenticity of received notions of what constitutes significant delivery of information.

Carver's suspicion of language, although its manifestation is understated when compared with the radical innovations of the postmodernists, reflects his social outlook and also has something to do with his trusting in fragments. Typically attributed to Donald Barthelme, this creed is manifested quite differently by Carver: instead of overloading the page with a blizzard of cultural detritus the way Barthelme does, Carver abstains from verbal indulgence altogether. While Barthelme's proliferation of referents ends up leveling out all input, Carver's technique shows how even the most modest foray into the world at large overwhelms the ability to absorb anything at all. His initial interest in the short story may have been economically motivated—it provides quicker tangible rewards—but it exhibits the contours of his artistic philosophy:

To write a novel, it seemed to me, a writer should be living in a world that makes sense, a world that the writer can believe in, draw a bead on, and then write about accurately. A world that will, for a time anyway, stay fixed in one place. Along with this there has to be a belief in the essential *correctness* of that world. A belief that the known world has reasons for existing, and is worth writing about, is not likely to go up in smoke in the process. This wasn't the case with the world I knew and was living in.[10]

Coherence and communicability would constitute authorial arrogance, a betrayal of reality.

Taking this idea further, Carver chooses to investigate the uninspiring conditions under which meaning might be achieved these days. In other words, his prose defamiliarizes the daily—one feels as though he were trying to negotiate his cellar stairs in the dark—by holding for inspection what is typically consigned to the voiceless background of fiction. To create what Stanley Elkin calls "the strange displacements of the ordinary,"[11] Carver chooses the opposite tactic from Elkin's: he rejects the lavish for the lean. There are none of the luscious, coiling sentences of Elkin, William Gass, or John Hawkes in his landscape; to get the fish Carver drains the lake. The correlative in painting is superrealism, as seen in the polished gleam of Richard Estes's surfaces that are made alien by their insistent foregrounding.[12] In theater, where "minimalism" has greater currency as a critical term, there is the formidable example of Samuel Beckett's lifelong combat with the inexpressible and his reduction of stage event, property, and personality (in such play pieces as *Not I, Ohio Impromptu*, and *Breath*) to reach dramatic bedrock. Carver, too, believes in the richness of a glimpse and in the artistic legitimacy of being awestruck and left gaping by contemporary American life.

Carver probes into the furtive silences that lurk just behind the routines people keep. The dull captivity people endure in his stories is no guarantee of security. Underground streams of unease steal just beneath the narrative. If Carver's laconic surface is indebted to Hemingway, his atmosphere recalls Franz Kafka and Harold Pinter; the way someone pushes his food about the plate or hangs up the phone can be charged with menace. The tantalizing fragility of Carver's works is not due to a weak-willed abandonment of amplitude and depth, as some of his detractors suggest; rather, it results from his uncanny talent for catching lives at the moment they have begun to fray.

This brings to light another of Carver's "trademarks": the open-endedness, or lack of resolution, of his stories. "It would be inappropriate and, to a degree, impossible to resolve things neatly for these people and situations I'm writing about," Carver declares, going on to state that "satisfying" the reader's expectations and fulfilling the story's structural demands are by no means equivalent to providing unambiguous answers to the problems of plot.[13] Here, too, it is instructive to note how Carver's fiction parallels the notorious distrust of totalization observed by Mas'ud Zavarzadeh in *The Mythopoeic Reality* and evidenced throughout the terrain of postmodern fiction.[14] A principal lesson of the postmodernists is that epiphany is not something that is discovered in the world but created in the text; it does not originate from divine intervention but from literary convention, and self-evident works of art delight in exposing that contrivance to a sophisticated readership. Revelation is not a spiritual achievement but a linguistic one, and the role of language is not simply to commemorate the experience but to constitute it. Facing a worldly reality that, according to the consensus of recent fiction, is decentered and unsystematic at best and nonsensical at worst, the focused and stable meaning that epiphany suggests has been outdated for generations. A "totalizing fiction" which professes an integrated, even absolute, vision of reality is as antiquated as the myth of the hieratic author that it complements.

Carver is just as wary of granting his struggling characters any artificial lucidity or of rushing to restore composure to situations that have leaked out of hand. In his essay "On Writing" he observes, "What creates tension in a piece of fiction is partly the way the concrete words are linked together to make up the visible action of the story. But it's also the things that are left out, that are implied, the landscape just under the

CONNOISSEUR OF THE COMMONPLACE

smooth (but sometimes broken and unsettled) surface of things."[15] One recollects Robert Frost's paradoxical dictum: "All metaphor breaks down somewhere. That is the beauty of it."[16] That is also the truth of it. Healing the ruptures—the divorces, deaths, and disappointments, all the creeping doubts like private ghosts—would be aesthetically unconscionable, not to mention beyond the scope of the characters who suffer them in Carver's fiction. Thus, his endings are often abrupt, truncated. To illustrate, here are representative examples from his first collection, *Will You Please Be Quiet, Please?*:

> I feel depressed. But I won't go into it with her. I've already told her too much.
> She sits there waiting, her dainty fingers poking her hair.
> *Waiting for what?* I'd like to know.
> It is August.
> My life is going to change. I feel it.
>
> —*"Fat"*

> They stayed there. They held each other. They leaned into the door as if against a wind, and braced themselves.
>
> —*"Neighbors"*

> "Daddy doesn't look like *anybody!*" Alice said.
> "But he has to look like *somebody,*" Phyllis said, wiping her eyes with one of the ribbons. And all of them except the grandmother looked at the father, sitting at the table.
> He had turned around in his chair and his face was white and without expression.
>
> —*"The Father"*

She wet her lips with a sticking sound and got down on her knees. She put her hands out on the bed.

"God," she said. "God, will you help us, God?" she said.

— *"The Student's Wife"*

When he got back into bed, he moved closer to her and put his hand on her hip. "Hon, wake up," he whispered. But she only shuddered and moved over farther to her own side. She kept on sleeping. "Wake up," he whispered. "I hear something outside."

— *"The Ducks"*

"I hate tricks," Carver admits. "At the first sign of a cheap trick or a gimmick in a piece of fiction, a cheap trick or even an elaborate trick, I tend to look for cover."[17] While he appears to be echoing his mentor, John Gardner, whose *On Moral Fiction* is a book-length diatribe against what he considers stylistic preciousness and self-indulgent dazzle, Carver also appears to be referring to stories that sell out their difficulties for the comforts of closure. If postmodern fiction promotes a collaborative version of meaning that is elusive and negotiable, Carver's fiction is similarly collaborative, in that readers are challenged to complete for themselves the fragments that have been entrusted to them.

But it would be a mistake to glibly equate these achievements with artlessness, as though Carver's particular brand of realism were just the prose entry among such signs of the times as microwave ovens, computer chips, and Reaganomics. Carver strips the page to its essentials, down to the story's core. Where a Henry

CONNOISSEUR OF THE COMMONPLACE

James or a William Faulkner might endlessly delve, Carver merely hints. He constructs a life style out of a few mundane objects littering the room and charges the casual phrase with massive implication, blunt as a blackjack. ("I will show you fear in a handful of dust," warned T. S. Eliot in *The Waste Land*.) In an often cited passage Carver claims, "It's possible, in a poem or a short story, to write about commonplace things and objects using commonplace but precise language, and to endow those things—a chair, a window curtain, a fork, a stone, a woman's earring—with immense, even startling power."[18] Carver stays faithful to the gross tokens of American culture—the stuff of waitresses, fishermen, salesmen, mail carriers; like Saul Bellow's Augie March, he is "a sort of Columbus of those near at hand."[19] "Low-rent tragedies," as one Carver character calls them, seldom make the papers, so it is up to fiction to recover them.

To do so Carver abjures the "vague or blurred" and avoids "smoked-glass prose."[20] William Carlos Williams, another devoted chronicler of the importance and the futility of average Americans, advises that "the difficulty is to catch the evasive life of the thing, to phrase the words in such a way that stereotype will yield a moment of insight. That is where the difficulty lies."[21] The artist's dilemma is how to lift "to the imagination those things which lie under the direct scrutiny of the senses, close to the nose. It is this difficulty that sets a value upon all works of art and makes them a necessity."[22]

UNDERSTANDING RAYMOND CARVER

Raymond Carver helps ventilate the contemporary literary scene with his plain-dealing, "post-postmodern" style and consequent reavowal of extratextual reality. The world he addresses is defined by odd jobs and compromised aspirations. Carver is just as appreciative of what is no less valuable for being anonymous. In the words of John Gardner, whom Carver gratefully credits as a formative influence, "Art rediscovers, generation by generation, what is necessary to humanness."[23] Through a meticulous regard for how the plainest people live, Carver makes his own small-change world possible for art.

Notes

1. The majority of these terms and/or allegations are borrowed from Kim A. Herzinger, "Introduction: On the New Fiction," *Mississippi Review* 40/41 (Winter 1985): 8; and from John Barth, "A Few Words About Minimalism," *New York Times Book Review* 28 Dec. 1986: 2.

2. "Less Is Less," *Atlantic* June 1981: 97.

3. Barth 25.

4. Tom Jenks, an editor at *Esquire*, attests that "the style most often attempted by young writers is one marked by short, hard-edged sentences, like those of Raymond Carver, and the subject matter often brushes up against Carver's as well—representative of what I would call a downside neo-realism." Quoted in Bruce Weber, "Raymond Carver: A Chronicler of Blue-Collar Despair," *New York Times Magazine* 24 June 1984: 36.

CONNOISSEUR OF THE COMMONPLACE

5. *The Postmodern Aura: The Act of Fiction in an Age of Inflation.* *Salmagundi* 63–64 (Spring–Summer 1984): 93.

6. Charles Newman, "What's Left Out of Literature," *New York Times Book Review* 12 July 1987: 25.

7. Quoted in Larry McCaffery and Sinda Gregory, "An Interview with Raymond Carver," *Mississippi Review* 40/41 (Winter 1985): 74.

8. William H. Gass, "A Failing Grade for the Present Tense," *New York Times Book Review* 11 Oct. 1987: 35.

9. Herzinger 20.

10. "Fires," *Fires: Essays, Poems, Stories* (Santa Barbara: Capra, 1983) 26.

11. Stanley Elkin, *The Dick Gibson Show* (New York: Random, 1971) 7.

12. For further analysis of the congruities between prose and painting, see Jerome Klinkowitz, "Experimental Realism," *Postmodern Fiction: A Bio-Bibliographical Guide*, ed. Larry McCaffery (Westport, CT: Greenwood, 1986) 69–71.

13. Quoted in McCaffery and Gregory 76–77.

14. Mas'ud Zavarzadeh, *The Mythopoeic Reality: The Postwar American Nonfiction Novel* (Urbana: University of Illinois Press, 1976) 3–49.

15. "On Writing," *Fires* 17.

16. "Education by Poetry," quoted in Guy Rotella, "Comparing Conceptions: Frost and Eddington, Heisenberg, and Bohr," *American Literature* 59 (May 1987): 172.

17. "On Writing," in *Fires* 14. It is arguable, however, that Carver's own relentlessly subtractive style betrays evidence of gimmickry. As Alain Arias-Misson writes, "Carver has *not* given a voice to his characters; he has given his characters to a voice. The *voix blanche* turned inside out like a glove." In "Absent Talkers," *Partisan Review* 49 (1982): 627.

18. "On Writing," *Fires* 15.

19. *The Adventures of Augie March* (New York: Viking, 1953) 536.

20. "Fires," *Fires* 28.

21. *The Autobiography of William Carlos Williams,* quoted in Gilbert

Sorrentino, "The Various Isolated: W. C. Williams' Prose," *New American Review* 15 (1972): 207.

22. William Carlos Williams, quoted in M. L. Rosenthal, introduction, *The William Carlos Williams Reader*, ed. M. L. Rosenthal (New York: New Directions, 1966) xvi.

23. *On Moral Fiction* (New York: Basic Books, 1977) 6. In 1958 Gardner instructed Carver in a beginning fiction writing course at Chico State College. Carver acknowledges and details the nature of his debt to Gardner in "Fires" (27–9).

CHAPTER TWO

Will You Please Be Quiet, Please?

"They're Not Your Husband," "Are You a Doctor?" "Nobody Said Anything," "What's in Alaska?" "What Do You Do in San Francisco?" "Why, Honey?" "How About This?" "What Is It?" The preponderance of titles in Carver's first major collection of short stories[1] (originally published during the early 1960s to the mid-1970s) are pulled from ordinary discourse, but they have the effect of distress signals. If the phrasings are unremarkable, their urgency cannot be underestimated. Most telling in this regard may be the title that heads the volume and connotes both the ineffectuality and the threat of communication. Intimacy is either impossible to achieve or too terrible to bear. "Will You Please Be Quiet, Please?" is reminiscent of the conversation-killer in Hemingway's "Hills Like White Elephants": "Would you please please please please please please please stop talking?"[2] Carver's characters are victims of anguishes they can neither brave nor name, only suffer. William Carlos Williams's diagnosis

21

in *Paterson* targets them exactly: "The language is missing them / they die also / incommunicado."[3]

Shocked to whispers, they manifest this common malady in a variety of misguided outbursts, neuroses, and perversions as they try to hold on. "In a time of troubles," writes Christopher Lasch in *The Minimal Self: Psychic Survival in Troubled Times*,

everyday life becomes an exercise in survival. . . . Under these conditions, selfhood becomes a kind of luxury, out of place in an age of impending austerity. Selfhood implies a personal history, friends, family, a sense of place. Under siege, the self contracts to a defensive core, armed against adversity. Emotional equilibrium demands a minimal self, not the imperial self of yesteryear.[4]

Attempts to fortify the self throughout *Will You Please Be Quiet, Please?* frequently turn into missions of appropriation. Despairing of meaningful engagements, the protagonists become obsessed with vicariousness. They stake their fates on the hope that prospects are not so desolate on the other side. Thus they are more voyeuristic than visionary, for they barely hesitate to jeopardize their own identities in deference to petty intrigues or somewhat more exotic personalities.[5] Witnessed throughout the collection is a wholesale concession to the supremacy of otherness based upon the suspicion that true substance lies outside a terminally second-rate

WILL YOU PLEASE BE QUIET, PLEASE?

self. "I think most of my characters would like their actions to count for something," Carver explains.

> But at the same time they've reached the point—as so many people do—that they know it isn't so. It doesn't add up any longer. The things you once thought important or even worth dying for aren't worth a nickel now. It's their lives they've become uncomfortable with, lives they see breaking down. They'd like to set things right, but they can't.[6]

In some cases this results in an indefinable sense of frustration, but it can also be a prelude to self-annihilation.

Because Carver's locations are unexceptional, they are deceptively lulling, seemingly immune to eventfulness; yet all the while, in familiar homes and neighborhoods, acts of brinkmanship regularly take place. What, for example, could be less precipitous than a waitress serving a customer? Yet in "Fat" the event looms monumentally in her consciousness. Breathless and repetitive, the narrator anxiously tries to "sell" her friend on the significance of the tale of her incredibly fat customer as if she had just been implicated in some vague parable. However, she cannot pin down the reason for its having unsettled her so: "Now that's part of it. I think that is really part of it." "I know now I was after something. But I don't know what." "*Waiting for what?* I'd like to know."[7]

Perhaps it is the surprising dignity and pleasantness of the fat man that is so remarkable—one can easily surmise what sort of course treatment she is accustomed to—and that causes her to defend him against the rude remarks of her co-workers. Perhaps his use of the royal "we" to refer to himself, as though he needed to measure up verbally to his size, makes her realize how dwarfed and submissive she has been. Or perhaps the jokes about her being "sweet" on him lead her to reevaluate her relationship with Rudy, who is similarly incapable of appreciating feelings she can hardly approximate. (During their lovemaking, she imagines herself to be so astonishingly fat that Rudy disappears within her bulk.) Her inarticulateness stakes out the limits of her growth of consciousness. Significantly, although she believes her life will change—the meeting with the mysterious fat man surely heralds it—she still characterizes herself as passive, waiting for a transformation. "Fat" concludes with the narrator prepared for something different but at a loss as to what that "something" could be or how she would go about initiating it. Insight extends no further than dissatisfaction.

In "Neighbors" the Millers are similarly caught in the no-man's-land just outside the confines of a disqualified life style. They are deemed a happy couple until they compare their mundane existence with that of the Stones, whose jobs afford them travel opportunities and who fondle souvenirs in front of their neighbors. Meanwhile, the Millers (Bill is a bookkeeper, Arlene a secretary), who keep watch over the Stones' vacant apartment and feed their cat, suspect that they "had been passed by somehow" (7). Like the waitress in "Fat" they come to see themselves as relegated to attendance upon others more distinguished than they.

As the story progresses, Bill Miller begins to take peculiar advantage of his access to the apartment of the itinerant Stones. He rummages among their belongings, casually at first, but soon with criminal design. His parasitism ranges from petty thievery to trying on both Jim's and Harriet's clothes. To be sure, there is little in the Stones' apartment to indicate any special opulence; they are the Millers' neighbors, after all, and share the same building. However, Bill imagines the air to be cool and sweet there, and each incursion is a symbolic coup, a delicious revelry, and a vacation from himself. What is more, he returns home filled with sexual vigor. His wife also becomes addicted to the proximity of intrigue:

"It's funny," she said. "You know—to go in someone's place like that."

He nodded, took her hand from the knob, and guided her toward their own door. He let them into their apartment.

"It *is* funny," he said.

He noticed white lint clinging to the back of her sweater, and the color was high in her cheeks. He began kissing her on the neck and hair and she turned and kissed him back (13).

Galvanized by their sovereignty over the Stones, they indulge themselves by forgetting themselves. Their absurd hope that the Stones may not return—"Anything could happen," Bill says (13)—is dashed when they accidentally lock the keys inside the Stones' apartment. Shaken, they cling to one another, exposed and vulnerable as a postlapsarian Adam and Eve cast out of Paradise.

Provoked to voyeurism by a strange sexual ritual of their neighbors, the couple in "The Idea" find their fascination with what is going on next door more disturbing than what they actually witness: a man peers through his own window to watch his wife undress. The thrill for the central characters in this story is having a privileged vantage point, being the unwatched watchers. However, whereas the Millers in "Neighbors" were sexually invigorated by their practices, Vern and his wife just get "jumpy" and channel their anxieties into other appetites: eating or watching television. Nevertheless, their feigned indifference does not give them much consolation or sense of superiority over their neighbors. Not only are they as compulsive in their vigilance as the people they spy upon—as peeping Toms twice removed from the striptease, they may be even more peculiar and dubious than the husband they regularly analyze—but they reveal their own frailties in their comments on the proceedings. She wonders what could be the secret of that woman's appeal; he muses about whether his neighbor may have discovered the key to restoring excitement to life.

"The Idea" concludes with the infestation of their kitchen by ants, which imitates their own voyeuristic invasions. Although the woman sprays thoroughly, she cannot purge her imagination of the creatures. (A similar episode transforms the domestic consciousness of the wife in William Gass's "The Order of Insects" as "the consequence of finally coming near to something."[8]) Nor can she share her nervousness with her husband:

> Vern was asleep. He was snoring. He'd wake up in a few hours, go to the bathroom, and smoke. The little TV at the foot of the bed was on, but the picture was rolling.
> I'd wanted to tell Vern about the ants.
> I took my own time getting ready for bed, fixed the picture, and crawled in. Vern made the noises he does in his sleep (19).

As in "Fat," the greatest privation may be the inhibition that prevents communication. The comparative freedom to express themselves enjoyed by their neighbors is positively seductive in itself.

Prowling about the neighborhood jeopardizes one's own defenses against intrusion. Harold Pinter describes this fundamental crisis in a well-known formula:

> A man in a room and no one entering lives in expectation of a visit. He will be illuminated or horrified by the absence of a visitor. But however much

it is expected, the entrance, when it comes, is almost always unwelcome. (He himself, of course, might go out of the door, knock and come in and be his own visitor. It has happened before.)[9]

Although the interruption of life's rituals may seem as trivial from an objective stance as the rituals themselves, it is devastating nevertheless because the character in question views it that way.

In "They're Not Your Husband," Earl Ober is especially vulnerable to catastrophe because he is "between jobs," which means that he is failing to prove himself according to his own standards of accomplishment. When he visits his wife at the coffee shop where she works, he overhears crude remarks about her weight. A spasm of doubt runs through him. Earl does not reveal his identity or defend his wife; instead, he accepts the superimposition of the derisive perspective of her customers. He notices how "the white skirt yanked against her hips and crawled up her legs" as she bent over. "What showed was girdle, and it was pink, thighs that were rumpled and gray and a little hairy, and veins that spread in a berserk display" (21).

Removed from the context of routine acquaintance, Doreen suddenly becomes a problem to be corrected. Earl begins a regular clinical study of her, poking and measuring her naked body as though trying to divine the original source of her appeal. He cannot explain his unprecedented disappointment in Doreen's appearance: " 'I never felt it was a problem before,' he said. He tried to pick his words" (22). This is not his way of saving her feelings; he is as mystified as she is by his own behavior.

Whatever its subtler causes, Earl's comprehensive inventory of his wife has the effect of punishment. He carefully dockets her waitressing tips and lost pounds and condemns her to a starvation diet. When he catches her sneaking food on one occasion, he blows up at her treachery. Doreen meekly complains that her co-workers have commented on her pallor, but Earl is adamant: "Tell them to mind their own business. They're not your husband. You don't have to live with them" (25). Ironically, Earl has already contradicted this exclusive criterion of approval since his mania has been instigated by strangers. Furthermore, once his wife's diet has had discernible results, he returns to the site of his earlier humiliation seeking confirmation of his new stature. He tries to solicit reactions to Doreen from the man next to him at the counter: "Don't you think that's something special?" and "Does it look good or not?" he prods, nosing about for validation of his reclamation project. (The sexually adventurous couple in "The Idea" also invited outside analysis, but one may assume that they were both in on the plan.) Getting no response, Earl intensifies his "exhibitionism" by vulgarly accosting the "desirable piece," but he comes off as pathetic, not impressive.

Earl gets his comeuppance in a sense when Doreen returns the compliment of treating him, at least initially, as a stranger.

"Who is this joker, anyway?"

Earl put on his best smile. He held it. He held it until he felt his face pulling out of shape.

But the other waitress just studied him, and Doreen began to shake her head slowly. The man had put some change beside his cup and stood up, but he too waited to hear the answer. They all stared at Earl.

"He's a salesman. He's my husband," Doreen said at last, shrugging (28).

Thus she is as embarrassed by Earl as he had been by her at the beginning of the story. Once again Carver presents a couple who are ravaged by disappointments and misgivings and whose relationship is too tenuous to afford airing them. So they grow perverse, or petulant, or sullen, and silently apart.

"Are You a Doctor?" opens innocently enough with a wrong number. A divorced woman, Clara Holt, trying to contact a doctor for her sick child, accidentally calls the unlisted number of Arnold Breit, who has been awaiting his wife's call (she is a buyer out of town on business). Clara's urgency is captivating compared to an otherwise ordinary evening, and Arnold finds himself oddly drawn into an unexpected conspiracy of sorts. Having elicited his name, Clara repeats it like a talisman:

"I know I'm imposing, Arnold, but do you think we could meet somewhere we could talk? Just a few minutes."

"I'm afraid that's impossible," he said.

"Just for a minute, Arnold. My finding your
number and everything. I feel very strongly about
this."
"I'm an old man," he said.
"Oh, no you're not," she said (31).

Sinful visions aside, Arnold Breit (Honor Bright? an
embodiment of conventional trustworthiness?) is
convinced by the prospect of shedding the skin of pre-
dictability and rebelling against the role of
man-who-sits-dutifully-by-the-phone-waiting-for-his-
wife-to-call; "the temptation to dress himself in an alien
persona triumphs over middle-age inertia."[10]
    This lasts until he reaches her apartment building,
where he is seized by recriminations: "He felt a sudden
pain in his side, imagined his heart, imagined his legs
folding under him, imagined a loud fall to the bottom of
the stairs" (33). As it turns out, however, Clara's apartment is decidedly unromantic—drab, disarrayed, and
dominated by Clara's preoccupation with her child's
health. The "affair" dissipates before it starts; Clara can
hardly recall why she had implored Arnold to come in
the first place:

"Then there's nothing?" he said.
"No. I mean *yes.*" She shook her head. "What you
said, I mean. Nothing" (37).

The confused anticlimax insults Arnold's anticipation.
He tries in vain to rescue the transgression with an awk-

ward kiss, but once again, as in "Fat" and "Neighbors," arousal is followed by an indefinite deferral. Arnold's heightened sensibilities—he felt his heart beating and studied himself in the mirror for the first time before making the momentous decision to come here—have only brought him to an impasse.

When he returns home, the telephone rings again, and he responds fervently . . . but it is just his wife, who jokes about his having been out "living it up" (it could only be a joke in reference to her Arnold). Remanded to the old pattern, cheated out of his newly animated awareness of himself, Arnold grows noticeably aloof. " 'Are you there, Arnold?' she said. 'You don't sound like yourself' " (38). Carver leaves them on the verge of inevitable distance from one another.

Thus, when there is no imminent action to accompany it, self-revelation can terrorize instead of liberate. A glance at the mirror held too long, a moment's hesitation before getting the phone, or something out of place in the closet can strip away all the familiar upholstery of one's existence and turn a person into "his own visitor." Carver compresses this threat into a matter of seconds in the volume's shortest piece, "The Father." The female members of a family are hovering over the new baby and discussing whom the new baby resembles while the baby's father keeps to himself in the other room. After the observation that the baby looks like the father, the man who had been reliably swathed in his "Daddy identity" is thrust into the existential spotlight:

WILL YOU PLEASE BE QUIET, PLEASE?

"But who does Daddy *look* like?" Phyllis asked.

"Who does Daddy *look* like?" Alice repeated, and they all at once looked through to the kitchen where the father was sitting at the table with his back to them.

"Why, nobody!" Phyllis said and began to cry a little (40).

In another context the father's estrangement from the group could have been written off as his temporary displacement from the center of attention by the novel addition of a baby to the household; the question of "Who does Daddy look like" would have been a trifle. But Carver's vignette casts the father into a full-blown identity crisis, and looking like nobody is not a badge of uniqueness but a glimpse into a black hole. The daughter's sorrow is magnified into the father's shock. His face is "white and without expression," appalled and unrecognizable. "The Father" depicts an instantaneous confrontation with nothingness, as Carver nods to Alfred Hitchcock and Franz Kafka.

Although Carver himself does not specifically name Kafka among those writers for whom he feels special admiration,[11] one particular line from "Conversation with the Supplicant" defines a persistent paradox in Carver's stories: "You see, I have only such a fugitive awareness of things around me that I always feel they were once real and are now fleeting away. I have a constant longing, my dear sir, to catch a glimpse of things as they may have been before they show themselves to me. I feel that then they were calm and beautiful."[12] A dream of access to a pristine world free of guilt and frustration lies behind the desperate activities in *Will You Please Be Quiet, Please?* Part of the dream's undoing may be the fact that Carver's characters often resort to the outrageous—voyeurism, sexual duplicity, or other strategies to escape the contaminants of self-consciousness—to achieve that freedom. But even the splendors of the natural world, traditionally dependable as a means of transcending the dull rigors of the everyday, prove unavailing. On those occasions when Carver's characters manage to extricate themselves from their rooms to go hunting or fishing, they usually learn that the realities they have sought to leave behind still enclose them.

In "Nobody Said Anything" the young narrator hopes to escape the constant combat between his parents by reviving his idyllic memories of fishing at Birch Creek. The title is a refrain throughout the story that at once names the common response to hardship and serves as its principal symptom. Counterparts of the adults, the boys are also constantly at each other. But unlike his brother, whose callousness and profanity armor him against the sounds of the fighting of the parents (he is "a royal asshole" with the privileges of insensitivity that that stature allows), the narrator takes every harsh word he overhears as if it were a blow struck at him. The child's difficulty in expressing himself makes his suffering seem that much more acute:

WILL YOU PLEASE BE QUIET, PLEASE?

After a while she came to call us to school. Her voice sounded funny—I don't know. I said I felt sick at my stomach. It was the first week in October and I hadn't missed any school yet, so what could she say? She looked at me, but it was like she was thinking of something else (41).

She is too distraught, too exhausted, to take on her son, so she lets him stay home.

When he is alone, the boy takes his cue from the Millers in "Neighbors" and searches through his parents' belongings for intimations of their sex life (he is formidably obsessed with this topic) or for money they would not miss. Then he decides to go fishing at Birch Creek.

He hitches a ride along the way from a woman who fuels his fantasies of a more momentous encounter, but he is embarrassed by a growing erection and ultimately chides himself for his failure to be more aggressive. (Of course, the reason she stopped to pick him up was that he presented no danger.) So he tries to focus on the fishing expedition. He conjures the memory of a roaring river, an abundant catch, and easy comraderie with his brother and father. Unfortunately the reality of Birch Creek is another letdown: it is late in the season, the river is sunken, oily tire marks surround the flowers. Feeling "jinxed," he tries a few casts and works on his imaginary sex scene.

He gets a strike, but the trout is lethargic, and he can barely get any play out of it. The trout turns out to be a weird, green fish like none he had ever seen before: "He was fat, and I wondered why he hadn't put up more of a fight. I wondered if he was all right. I looked at him for a time longer, then I put him out of his pain" (50).

Only as he is about to give up the day does a real chance for valor arise. He encounters another boy, who has located a huge steelhead that he cannot manage alone. Seeing it himself, the narrator becomes feverishly excited and lets loose a flood of passionate invective that probably matches anything he has ever heard at home; his mixture of worship and menace is like his most violent sexual fantasies. He takes charge of the plan, which requires that the other boy kick the fish out of the riffle as it shoots by, but his rather obtuse companion, who mostly complains about not having brought his gun for the occasion, ends up lunging uselessly into the water. However, their next attempt to land the fish with their bare hands succeeds:

> We were wet and shivering. We looked at him, kept touching him. We pried open his big mouth and felt his rows of teeth. His sides were scarred, whitish welts as big as quarters and kind of puffy. There were nicks out of his head around his eyes and on his snout where I guess he had banged into the rocks and been in fights. But he was so skinny, too skinny for how long he was, and you could hardly see the pink stripe down his sides, and his belly was gray and slack instead of white and solid like it should have been. But I thought he was something (55).

WILL YOU PLEASE BE QUIET, PLEASE?

The fish is at once a prodigious phallic symbol for a boy who prizes potency, a chance to impress the adults, and a kind of saving grace; but, the other boy is just as covetous of their catch. The narrator suspects that he could defeat him in combat over it, but he does not want to sully the event that way. They negotiate and halve the fish, with the second boy receiving the tail portion and the green trout the narrator had gotten before.

The blissful pioneer returns home in triumph. He barges in on yet another argument, but he is secure in the belief that somehow his victory will not only establish his manhood but also rescue his family from their malaise. But the sight of the dripping half of the monstrous fish disgusts and enrages his parents:

He screamed, "Take that goddamn thing out of here! What in the hell is the matter with you? Take it the hell out of the kitchen and throw it in the goddamn garbage!"
I went back outside. I looked into the creel. What was there looked silver under the porch light. What was there filled the creel.
I lifted him out. I held him. I held that half of him (59).

Suddenly he is disqualified, holding garbage. How can he reconcile himself to the unmagical character of their lives now?

Lee Waite's distress in "Sixty Acres" unfolds against the backdrop of racial dispossession. Waite feels as much burdened as justified by his Indian heritage and the reservation territory it guarantees him. He wishes he did not have to respond to the call about trespassing duck hunters on his land because it threatens to expose the breakdown of his authority. Worse than an annoyance, then, it is another reproach, much like the invidious silence of his ancient mother, whose cryptic presence looms like judgment over the Waite household.

Waite's boys are eager "to know if this time he was going to shoot somebody. It bothered him, kids talking like that, like they would enjoy it" (61), and the conversation strikes him as if it were part of a conspiracy to mock his waning resources. Only sluggishly, reluctantly, does he set out. His pride is too obsolete to defend; rather, he is performing a distasteful duty, which is as useless as his habit of locking his gate although he no longer owns any horses.

Waite hopes that the intruders will be gone by the time he arrives, as is typically the case, but he has a presentiment of unavoidable trouble this time. On his way to investigate the reports of shooting, he remembers the violent deaths of his brothers that ended up saddling him with the dubious legacy of the sixty acres: "Lee Waite was the one it came down to, all of it" (65). Their "desertion" has also contributed to the conspiracy to root him to this unpromising spot.

He surprises two boys and interrogates them at gunpoint about their crime, but despite their predicament it is Waite himself who feels most uneasy. His

WILL YOU PLEASE BE QUIET, PLEASE?

questions are really stalling tactics; he wants to assert himself, to exact some sort of indefinable payment, but he knows all along that he will let them go. The thought of the dozens who have gotten away with this before and the boys' desperate lies about their real names increase his frustration, shocking him with the extent of his anger. The fact that he has retrieved their kill and expelled them is overshadowed by his admission that he would have had to help them out if their car battery had been dead.

He had put them off the land. That was all that mattered. Yet he could not understand why he felt something crucial had happened, a failure.
But nothing had happened (70).

There is no triumph for such an inveterate victim.
Back at the house Waite feels cramped and restless. His wife confesses that she had been afraid for him during his absence—the Waites have a family history of tragic news, after all—and Waite is too preoccupied to console her:

"I let them go," he said. "Maybe I was easy on them."
"You did what was right," Nina said.
He glanced over the stove at his mother. But there was no sign from her, only the black eyes staring at him.

"I don't know," he said. He tried to think about it, but already it seemed as if it had happened, whatever it was, long ago (71–2).

"I could've killed them," he reasons. Is it a sobering revelation of the depth of his rage or a complaint about a missed option?

As a practical surrender to the inevitable, Lee and Nina try to rationalize the possibility of leasing out the land to hunting clubs the way others on the reservation had already done. It would not be a capitulation, for it would not be the same as selling the land outright; however, since they *cannot* sell reservation land, the distinction is moot. Meanwhile, Waite's mother appears to be sleeping through their discussion and neither sanctions nor condemns. In this way, like the Millers outside their neighbors' locked door, the flustered Breits in "Are You a Doctor?" and the disenfranchised boy in "Nobody Said Anything," the Waites are left groping for reassurances. Waite feels as if the floor is shifting beneath him. The meagerness of his victories—the ouster of the trespassers and the plot to make a thousand dollars from leasing the land—only invalidates his imagined prospects.

The assault on stability in "What's in Alaska?" is even subtler as still another frontier is foreclosed. The slow-motion collapse of Carl and Mary is at once characterized and confirmed by the exasperating aimlessness of their interchanges. A critical juncture in their lives has been reached because she expects to receive an offer of a job in Fairbanks, but they avoid serious consideration of the possibility. The utterly prosaic opening of the story, in which Carl selects a new pair of shoes, belies the importance of the impending move—his purchase surely pales before her news—and yet they retain a maddeningly matter-of-fact atmosphere between them, preferring a superficial conversation about what junk food to buy on the way to Helen and Jack's.

Ritualistic avoidance continues at their friends' house. Smoking pot from a water pipe and gorging themselves on chips, popsicles, and cream soda help to ensure the reign of superficiality; significant subjects would be indecorous, and "heaviness" would be a "bummer." Guarding against the inadvertent offense, they court oblivion together, which no hard question can violate. Sufficiently glazed, they can erase their respective worries for a while and believe in love and providence. However, the temperate climate is troubled as, under the influence of the drugs, their censors falter:

"Alaska?" Jack said. "What's in Alaska? What would you do up there?"

"I wish we could go someplace," Helen said.

"What's wrong with here?" Jack said. "What would you guys do in Alaska? I'm serious. I'd like to know."

Carl put a potato chip in his mouth and sipped his cream soda. "I don't know. What did you say?"

After a while, Jack said, "What's in Alaska?"

"I don't know," Carl said. "Ask Mary. Mary
knows. Mary, what am I going to do up there?" (82).

Otherwise negligible incidents become teasingly
symbolic. Carl spies Mary with her arms around Jack,
and she accidentally refers to Jack as "Honey": is something going on between them, or are they just stoned?
Mary recounts the story of a prehistoric man discovered
in a block of ice: is it a premonition of Carl's fate, a
description of his current stasis, or just a confused
memory of something she read in the paper? Carl says,
"There's nothing in Alaska" and "There's nothing to do
in Alaska" (85), but perhaps he is just upset about spill-
ing soda on his new shoes, and anyway, he was on a
bummer when he came in that evening. The cat wanders in with a dead mouse, which he proceeds to lick
from head to tail, and disgust nullifies the effects of the
marijuana.

On the way home Carl's obsession with the state of
his shoes grows unaccountably. Meanwhile, Mary's desire to be numbed has become more insistent, even
frantic: " 'When we get home, Carl, I want to be
fucked, talked to, diverted. Divert me, Carl. I need to be
diverted tonight.' She tightened her hold on his arm"
(89). Sex, drugs, the dream of a better life, the fiction of
greener pastures even in the frozen North, and the eter-
nal Second Chance: one will do as well as another. If
spiritual blight cannot be cured, perhaps it can be
staved off or ignored.

WILL YOU PLEASE BE QUIET, PLEASE?

But anxiety will out. "What's in Alaska," Mary says, echoing her husband's concern as she falls asleep. Then Carl notices something vaguely predatory in the blackened hallway:

He kept staring and thought he saw it again, a pair of small eyes. His heart turned. He blinked and kept staring. He leaned over to look for something to throw. He picked up one of his shoes. He sat straight up and held the shoe with both hands. He heard her snoring and set his teeth. He waited. He waited for it to move once more, to make the slightest noise (91).

Whether it is a hallucination or an intuition of being at bay, the reader suspects that Carl is no match for it. Once again Carver's "hunter" feels hunted, inadequate to deal with his fears no matter how they are manifested from one story to the next: trespassers, wrong numbers, reflections in a mirror, or eyes waiting in the darkness. Carver exits at the moment the footsteps are heard.

"Night School" conforms to the politics of resignation that dominate the collection so far. Certainly the barren outlook that opens the story severely limits the protagonist's potential for an extraordinary destiny:

My marriage had just fallen apart. I couldn't find a job. I had another girl. But she wasn't in town. So I was at a bar having a glass of beer, and two women were sitting a few stools down, and one of them began to talk to me (92).

So denuded is his life that even the automatic amenities of bar conversation exhaust him. His halting manner is in keeping with his limbo state: thirty cents in his pocket, wifeless, companionless, no car, no occupation, no schedule, no impetus. One thinks of James Purdy's Malcolm or of John Barth's Jacob Horner, who are similarly devoid of intrinsic purposefulness and are therefore entirely given up to the plots of more substantial egos.[13]

The two women at the bar, "on the loose" for the evening, "abduct" the nameless hero into their plan to drop in unexpectedly at the home of their night school teacher. (The young man had gone to night school himself for a time, but, as might have been expected, his dedication dried up.) The insult of being relegated to a supporting role as chauffeur in this intrigue is compounded by the humiliation of having to borrow his father's car. Still, he cannot muster any complaint or comment.

The fledgling action of the story ceases when the father refuses to let his son go, telling him that he doesn't want to get "mixed up with that." His son not only anticipates this refusal, he seems almost relieved by it and admits that he is not going anywhere anyway. After all, he is used to anticlimax. For example, when one day he recounted a terrifying nightmare to his wife, she was indifferent and coldly dismissive. And now his

WILL YOU PLEASE BE QUIET, PLEASE?

father returns to watching his television, while the two women, who have been waiting outside his house for some time, curse him and leave. He quickly relapses into the security of anonymity and automatism:

> I went into the bathroom for a long time and then I went upstairs and let myself out. It was cooler, and I did up the zipper on my jacket. I started walking to Paul's. If I got there before my mother went off duty, I could have a turkey sandwich. After that I could go to Kirby's newsstand and look through the magazines. Then I could go to the apartment to bed and read the books until I read enough and I slept (99).

In "Are You a Doctor?" Arnold Breit was denied his breakthrough; in "Night School" the protagonist is rescued from it.

"Collectors" looks in on one more character who seems powerless to be born. Mr. Slater is out of work and shunning bill collectors, so he hides behind his curtains and keeps anxious vigil for the mailman to bring news of a supposed job up north. While other characters in *Will You Please Be Quiet, Please?* peer surreptitiously at other lives, Slater is a voyeur watching himself.

Slater's inevitable infiltrator is no bill collector, but he does symbolically call Slater to account. Aubrey Bell is the garrulous vacuum cleaner salesman who barges in with practiced chatter that hits Slater with intimate accuracy:

You'll be surprised to see what can collect in a mattress
over the months, over the years. Every day, every
night of our lives, we're leaving little bits of ourselves,
flakes of this and that, behind. Where do they go,
these bits and pieces of ourselves? Right through the
sheets and into the mattress, *that's* where! Pillows,
too. It's all the same (103).

Methodically ferreting through the house, Bell tries to
draw in as many of the fugitive "bits and pieces" of his
prospective customer as he can. He particularly roots
about for Slater's name, selfhood's last stand. Slater
parries Bell as best he can, arguing that his wife, who
had won the free home demonstration, no longer lives
there, but Bell is undeterrable and indisposable. (The
reader assumes that the desertion of the unseen wife in
"Night School" also made her a winner by comparison
to the claustrophobic person she left behind.) When
Slater pleads that he has no money to spare for a vacuum cleaner, he merely exposes himself as beggared
and grubby; to be sure, he does get reduced to whatever has been trapped in the filter of Bell's machine.
Slater is a vacuum that needs cleaning, and Bell has
materialized to verify and remove the debris.

Like Lee Waite in "Sixty Acres," Slater feels inevitably outmanned. Holding to his premises does nothing
to stave off vacancy. No Mr. Slater lives there.[14] Therefore, it is only fitting that when the awaited letter falls
through the front door mail slot, Bell snares it without
comment or objection from Slater: "Twice I started for

the letter. But he seemed to anticipate me, cut me off, so to speak, with his hose and his pipes and his sweeping and his sweeping. . . " (106). Snatching Slater's name, which Slater has refused to own up to anyway, he also makes off with his future. Slater succeeds in removing the intruder without having to buy anything, but his triumph is as illusory as Waite's in having expelled the duck hunters. With professional, parabolic absoluteness, Bell has taken Slater for all he is worth.

The title "What Do You Do in San Francisco?" immediately recalls "What's in Alaska?" for both questions, however innocently intended, turn out to be urgent demands for justification. As in "Collectors," here is someone waiting for a letter that will bring him out of his inertia, making him another of Carver's candidates for the undistinguished category e. e. cummings referred to as "mostpeople": "What do mostpeople mean by 'living'? They don't mean living. They mean the latest and closest plural approximation to singular prenatal activity. . . . "[15]

"What Do You Do in San Francisco?" is narrated by Henry Robinson, a mailman working in the small California town of Arcata. "This has nothing to do with me" (109), he begins, disclaiming any responsibility for the tale to follow. Indeed, his effrontery is far milder than that of Aubrey Bell in the previous story; it is more like blundering concern for a man he perceives as having been wronged in a manner Robinson can identify with.

When a "beatnik" family, the Marstons, arrive in Arcata, the mailman greets them with more than perfunctory interest, for they simply do not fit into the well-defined expectations of this staunchly working-class community. Robinson puzzles over their atrophy. Marston, always nervous in his presence, neither has nor seeks a job. The family never does unload the U-Haul trailer completely, nor does Marston ever get around to changing the name on the mailbox. The three kids roam freely, while the negligent young woman makes Robinson feel altogether awkward, which "was one of the things helped turn me against her from the first" (111). The rumors percolate—Marston is a criminal on the lam, or his wife is a dope addict—but Robinson determines that, whatever the nature of their purgatory, it is her fault. He himself has been divorced for nearly twenty years and has not seen his children in nearly that long, so he takes no small satisfaction in transferring his antipathies to *this* woman: "put me down for saying she wasn't a good wife and mother" (110).

One day the woman leaves with another man and Marston languishes. Robinson can only intuit the details of the desertion or of the salvation Marston is hoping will come in the mail, but he grows more and more forward about offering his advice (in particular, that Marston might consider giving himself over to hard work) as he delivers each day's junk mail. Ultimately, Robinson brings the expected letter, and as Marston tries to muster the courage to confront its contents, Robinson cannot contain himself any longer:

WILL YOU PLEASE BE QUIET, PLEASE?

I called out, "She's no good, boy. I could tell that the minute I saw her. Why don't you forget her? Why don't you go to work and forget her? What have you got against work? It was work, day and night, work that gave me oblivion when I was in your shoes and there was a war on where I was." (118).

Marston is spooked by the man's advances and stops coming out to meet him. Soon afterward he also leaves town. Robinson closes off the story by reaffirming the blessing of having work to engage his thoughts. He had been moved to relate the story of the Marstons by a newspaper account of a man who had been arrested near San Francisco for killing his wife and her boyfriend with a baseball bat. The man was not Marston, but the situation was similar enough to occasion the comparison. Even though he does not say so, Robinson probably approves of that man's relative forthrightness in handling his problems. "What Do You Do in San Francisco?" is not only Robinson's contribution to the gossip being perpetrated throughout Arcata about the strangers from the big city, but is also his effort to rationalize his own snooping as commiseration and to manipulate the few details about the Marstons at his disposal into supporting evidence for his personal philosophies regarding the treacheries of love and the compensations of oblivion.

Some of Carver's characters are throttled by personal limitations; others are stuck in the custody of a chafing marriage—a false asylum of good intentions. "The Student's Wife" is a title that demotes the main character to an appendage of her husband's inadequacies. The instability of their relationship is revealed through the grudging availability they provide one another. He reads Rainer Maria Rilke to her, which could be a relief from her child-care chores were it not for his primary concern with his own sonorousness, as he chants on heedlessly after she has dozed off. When an upsetting dream consumes her, he finds it too trying to listen. This is no less disturbing than the climax of the dream itself:

"You and I started arguing about who was going to sacrifice and sit all cooped up in the back. You said you were, and I said I was. But I finally squeezed in the back of the boat. It was so narrow it hurt my legs, and I was afraid the water was going to come in over the sides. Then I woke up."

"That's some dream," he managed to say and felt drowsily that he should say something more. "You remember Bonnie Travis? Fred Travis' wife? She used to have *color* dreams, she said" (122).

The same territorial psychology operates in "The Idea," in which the woman is loath to voice her aversive vision of the ants to the snoring Vern.

Now that a night's insomnia has exacerbated her condition, she keeps goading him awake for food, massage, and company. But his aloofness and exasperation at having to sacrifice his own sleep increase her distress and make their distance obvious. For example, he jokes about her "growing pains" when she asks to be rubbed:

> "Didn't you ever feel yourself growing?"
> "Not that I remember," he said (124).

If growth is foreign to him, so is aspiration. She invents a game of listing her "likes," but it shifts subtly into a prolonged expression of desire in the conditional tense. In contrast to the numerous specific changes she accumulates, his imagination is bare:

"You're asleep," she said.
> "I'm not," he said.
> "I can't think of anything else. You go now. Tell me what you'd like."
> "I don't know. Lots of things," he mumbled.
> "Well, tell me. We're just talking, aren't we?"
> "I wish you'd leave me alone, Nan" (126).

Inarticulateness compounds his futility. His obstinate rhythms, awake and asleep, make her insomnia critical. In lieu of compassion from her husband, Nan scours the house for occupation and even summons the help of God, but nothing staves off the impact of the "terrible" sunrise that concludes her solitary, sleepless night. Were she to page through her husband's collection of Rilke, she might have come across "The Archaic Torso of Apollo," which ends, "You have to change your life."[16]

For all his vaunted awareness of people who cringe in their own shadows, Carver seldom satirizes. "God, the country is filled with these people. They're good people. People doing the best they could."[17] "Attention, attention must be finally paid to such a person" is the demand Linda makes on behalf of her husband, Willie Loman, in *Death of a Salesman*,[18] and Carver grants that respect to salesmen, cab drivers, and filling station attendants alike. But in "Put Yourself in My Shoes" he indulges his wit on behalf of a woefully misappreciated writer and at the expense of a couple of brusque philistines.

Myers is the man in Carver's shoes, a struggling author who is at once admired and suspected for having repudiated his office job for the tenuousness of writing fiction. At present his day is taken up with housecleaning and car troubles, for he is between stories, which is the artist's version of the state of abeyance witnessed throughout *Will You Please Be Quiet, Please?* To dispel the gloom, which is intensified by old-fashioned Christmas-season depression, Myers and his wife pay an unannounced visit to the Morgans, the owners of the house the Myerses had occupied during the Morgans' year in Germany.

When they arrive Myers falls on the ice, where he is immediately accosted by the Morgans' snarling dog. The dog's instincts are right enough in that these are the same people who had abused the privilege of staying there by opening sealed boxes, breaking dishes, and using forbidden linen. Thus, the voyeurism motif arises again; moreover, the self-reflective focus on writing-as-appropriation in "Put Yourself in My Shoes" may indict the profession itself for this offense. The balance of the story covers the strained hospitality of the Morgans toward the interlopers who have returned to the scene of their crimes. Morgan exercises his indignation by superciliously clumping about Myers's domain. He holds forth for his guests, telling stories on the pretext that Myers might appreciate their value:

"It's a horrible story, really. But maybe you could use it, Mr. Myers" (138).

"It would take a Tolstoy to tell it and tell it *right*," Morgan said. "No less than a Tolstoy" (140).

"You'll have another one, Mrs. Myers?" Morgan said, standing in front of her now with his hand on her cup. "You'll set an example for your husband."
"It *was* good," Paula said. "It warms you."
"Right," Morgan said. "It warms you. That's right. Dear, did you hear Mrs. Myers? It warms you. That's very good" (140).

As the evening drags on, it becomes clear that Mrs. Morgan is also tyrannized by the pomposity of her husband. For example, the carolers outside vex him, and his wife's prediction that they will not come by their house—do the Morgans ever receive visitors of any kind?—makes him vicious. Eventually the Myerses try to extricate themselves; however, Morgan is not finished with them. He insists on telling another story for their benefit about a woman who, having found and returned Mrs. Morgan's purse, drops dead right on the premises and is discovered to have stolen money from the purse. Mrs. Morgan's purple crescendo—"Fate sent her to die on the couch in our living room" (146)—not only renders the tragedy ludicrous, it tickles Myers so that he cannot restrain his laughter. Morgan unleashes his outrage:

"If you were a real writer, as you say you are, Mr. Myers, you would not laugh," Morgan said as he got to his feet. "You would not dare laugh! You would try to understand. You would plumb the depths of that poor soul's heart and try to understand. But you are no writer, sir!" (147).

He goes on to assail him with his rendition of their destruction of property. Spurred my Myers's glee, he gets so carried away by his own vehemence that he accuses Myers of having stolen his jazz records, despite his wife's reminder that they have been lost since before the Myerses had lived there.

With Morgan ranting on, the Myerses rush out, scaring the dog in the process. In this way they take a kind of vengeance on the dog that the Morgans are denied against them. More importantly, Myers has apparently overcome his writer's block. Not the tales proffered by their hosts, but the tale *of* their hosts, whose treatment constitutes "Put Yourself in My Shoes," has salvaged Myers from the deadlock from which precious few of the characters in Carver's collection are ever liberated.

"Put Yourself in My Shoes" proves to be a brief respite. "Jerry and Molly and Sam" plunges the reader back into the realm of the chronically maladjusted. Al is trying to fend off calamities on every front: layoffs at Aerojet, overdue payments on the house and car, an oppressive home life. His insecurities touch off Prufrockian ruminations:

Now he was having an *affair*, for Christ's sake, and he didn't know what to do about it. He did not want it to go on, and he did not want to break it off: you don't throw everything overboard in a storm. Al was drifting, and he knew he was drifting, and where it was all going to end he could not guess at. But he was beginning to feel he was losing control over everything. Everything. Recently, too, he had caught himself thinking about old age after he'd been constipated a few days—an affliction he had always associated with the elderly. Then there was the matter of the tiny bald spot and of his having just begun to wonder how he would comb his hair a different way. What was he going to do with his life? he wanted to know.

He was thirty-one (152).

Al's decision to do away with Suzy, the family dog, stems from this fear of personal attrition and represents an effort to concentrate his complaints to a scale he can accommodate. In a rapacious world it is either victimize or be victimized, and like Edward Albee's Jerry in *Zoo Story*, Al chooses to face off against a dog because humans overmatch him. He justifies his treachery as the first step out of chaos.

Of course, Al acts surreptitiously. Since his love affair has fostered the habit of lying to his wife, he cannot get out of the house anymore without enduring a clash of tempers. "His life had become a maze, one lie overlaid upon another until he was not sure he could untangle them if he had to" (154). For this fact, too, Suzy is his scapegoat.

Wary of the potential shame of being caught during the act of abandonment—how much longer does he expect to get away with his adulterous abandonment of his family?—and wanting Suzy to be found and cared for in the end, Al drives out to his old neighborhood. If only he could have a dog's chance at indiscriminate acceptance, he thinks, he would never go back. If only the same safe bastion were accessible to him!

He wished he could keep driving and driving tonight until he was driving onto the old bricked main street of Toppenish, turning left at the first light, then left again, stopping when he came to where his mother lived, and never, never, for any reason ever, ever leave again (158).

WILL YOU PLEASE BE QUIET, PLEASE?

Al completes his mission, but to little avail, for the sense of pressure is not relieved. He goes to a local bar, where he buys pizza for a girl he meets; however, since he fails to pick her up, he counts the incident as just another expense against him. Next he visits his lover, who seems to be accustomed to mothering him through his travails. In fact, instead of romancing him, she grooms him for blackheads, and the effect is demeaning, not consoling.

Al comes home to the crisis of the lost dog, and the full weight of his callousness comes crashing down upon him:

Everything was going to hell. While he was shaving, he stopped once and held the razor in his hand and looked at himself in the mirror: his face doughy, characterless—*immoral*, that was the word. He laid the razor down. *I believe I have made the gravest mistake this time. I believe I have made the gravest mistake of all.* He brought the razor up to his throat and finished (163–64).

The quest to locate the dog becomes the key to restoring the family sanity and his last chance to save himself from ruin: "A man who would get rid of a little dog wasn't worth a damn. That kind of man would do anything, would stop at nothing" (165). After a desperate search he finds her; they regard one another and then the dog moves off. Al tells himself that some dogs are incorrigible, that Suzy's nature is not his fault, but he will have to bear the brunt of this failure too.

Al's attempts to resist victimization strangle him in a web of deceit. But the alternative to being a poor liar is not necessarily being honest, but being a proficient liar. "Why, Honey?" introduces a character who thrives on it; having mastered the talent for lying as a child, he matures into a social, if not moral, success.

"Why, Honey?" is delivered as a letter from his mother in response to someone, a diligent reporter or an agent in her son's employ, who has managed to learn her whereabouts. She charts her son's history of double-dealing and violence. He lies religiously, sometimes simply to hone his "craft," sometimes to conceal some betrayal (skipping school or quitting his job) or some unexplained hideousness (he appears to have murdered the cat, and his mother uncovers his blood-soaked shirt stuffed in the trunk of the car). Whenever she would venture to question him, he would either grow stony or accuse her of spying. The title question brings out a monster: "He didn't say anything, he kept staring, then he moved over alongside me and said I'll show you. Kneel is what I say, kneel down is what I say, he said, that's the reason why" (173). That he is also an exceptional student merely makes his delinquency more ambiguous, his threat more complex.

Then comes the discovery that he has become governor; it would have been less astounding to learn of his having become a gangster. Perhaps Carver implies that at this level of accomplishment the two merge, or that the power politics associated with being a victimizer instead of a victim mandate the same manner of ruthlessness regardless of what "career" one chooses. Meanwhile, the mother resembles Slater in "Collectors," the young man in "Night School," and Carl in "What's in Alaska?" in that she detests attention but is wasting in her burrow.

"The Ducks" repeats the lesson that no one is disaster-proof. A woman's vague disquiet turns out to be a presentiment of misfortune: her husband's boss at the mill dies without warning. At first this only means that the protagonist will have to cancel his plans to go duck hunting and that he will be home from work for the day. Eventually he and his wife begin to reflect on their own fragility, for every "death threat" must be taken personally. Whereas the mailman in "What Do You Do in San Francisco?" would likely have advised that the man lose himself in his work, he must resort to the refuge of muddled domesticity—television, eating, smoking, reading, all anxious ceremonies to preserve his composure. But his restlessness only increases. Maybe they could go away somewhere together, he tells his wife, but there is nowhere to go that tragedy could not surprise them.

The same theme of the inescapable verdict of death is investigated in "Harry's Death" in Carver's *Fires*. If anonymity is no defense against death in "The Ducks," neither is a reputation for splendor. Harry "was sharp too and somehow he could always work it around so that in any deal he came out smelling like a rose"; nevertheless, his fate refutes this: "He'd been places and done things, Harry had. Now he was dead."[19] The narrator of "Harry's Death" actually does run away to Mexico with Harry's daughter, whom he marries, but there is no eluding death's gravitational pull: she is killed in a boating accident.

As for the man in "The Ducks," his discomfiture is made that much more oppressive by its resistance to definition. When he attempts to make love to his wife—a burst of vitality to keep the blood moving—the effect of death's striking so close to home stops him cold:

He tried to think how much he loved her or if he loved her. He could hear her breathing but he could also hear the rain. They lay like this.
   She said, "If you don't want to, it's all right."
   "It's not that," he said, not knowing what he meant (181).

Like the woman in "The Student's Wife" and Carl, who in "What's in Alaska?" thinks he sees those tiny eyes waiting for him in the dark, he ends up unable to sleep and feeling hunted. Whatever lurks outside in "The Ducks" may be something horrifying or supernatural; most probably it is as common as mortality.

The couple in "How About This?" actually do try to change their lives, with uncertain results. By making a romantic dash to the country, a dilettantish writer and his would-be artist-wife seek to establish a fresh start for themselves. Unfortunately, her father's deserted

WILL YOU PLEASE BE QUIET, PLEASE?

house in northwestern Washington is not poetic, just dilapidated. He is more edgy than hopeful, and she is more querulous than confident. Although they conspire to think well of their prospects, they cannot sustain any optimism for long:

He rapped on the walls near the front door.
"Solid. A solid foundation. If you have a solid foundation, that's the main thing." He avoided looking at her. She was shrewd and might have read something from his eyes.
"I told you not to expect too much," she said.
"Yes, you did. I distinctly remember," he said, still not looking at her (186).

Their persistent gauging of one another, as their inspection of the house's foundation precipitates an examination of the foundation of their relationship, is more than they can afford to talk about openly. They cannot quite commit themselves to anything: a dwelling, a career, an embrace.

These furtive silences and shaky grounds are according to custom. But as he further explores his new habitat, the husband senses that here is a place that is not useless, but unused. Like the half-finished portrait of the man and woman she has been working on, their fate awaits completion. When he decides to go back to the city, it is a victory of sorts if only because it *is* a decision and will necessitate the relinquishment of the pipedream of the writer he could have been (given a "proper" aesthetic environment). But as he prepares to tell his wife, he finds her doing cartwheels, reliving the first flush of the possible she had enjoyed as a child when she dreamed of being a high-wire artist. Her eager homily that they will "just have to love each other" must be tempered by his having decided against staying. "How About This?" ends before he has a chance to confess this, and, indeed, he may still vacillate. Will her fortified faith replenish the promise the place had originally held for him, or will his resignation win the day? They are left perched together on that precarious high wire and realize some solace from inconclusiveness.

"Bicycles, Muscles, Cigarettes" exhibits a tenderness and a cautious but compelling hopefulness that are rare in Carver's debut collection. Having just stopped smoking, Evan Hamilton is in a particularly brittle mood. A boy rides by the house with the news that Hamilton's son, Roger, is being held for questioning at his house regarding the loss of a bicycle Roger and his friends had borrowed from the boy's younger brother, Gilbert. Although he admits he would prefer that his wife respond to the summons, Hamilton feels that it is his place to go. Still, he anticipates that he will be getting out of his depth: "He hadn't known of the existence of this street and was sure he would not recognize any of the people who lived here. He looked around him at the unfamiliar houses and was struck with the range of his son's personal life" (195). In short, he is primed for a bout of defamiliarization; the strange house in Arbuckle Court will serve as the threshold to an unprecedented appreciation of his son and of the attitudes and responsibilities that comprise Evan Hamilton.

As Hamilton attempts to sort out the conflicting stories of who vandalized the bicycle and where it is now, the sniggering of the older boys (the likeliest culprits) in the next room, the crossfire of accusations and counteraccusations, and his craving for tobacco start him smoldering. The father of the second accused boy, Mr. Berman, a boorish, vindictive man, arrives on the scene, and the boys pair off with their respective fathers like fighters consulting with their corners between rounds. Berman's boy fires off blatant lies, and Berman adds a few contemptuous remarks of his own.

What is the full province of fatherhood? Is family solidarity more critical than justice? While Gilbert's mother grieves over her husband's absence, Hamilton and Berman square off. Hamilton amazes himself by tackling and pinning the larger man on the lawn. Meanwhile, the older boys pretend to box in the background; the third accused boy runs home to the reassuring company of his own father.

On their way home Roger asks to feel his father's muscle. Hamilton is chagrined, for he fears that the lesson he had wished to impart to his son—some paternal axiom about owning up to your wrongdoings or handling difficulties maturely—has been obliterated by the demonstration of the macho ethic of "might makes right." Indeed, Hamilton's vision of his own father has been molded in much the same way: "Hamilton had

loved his father and could recall many things about
him. But now he recalled his father's one fistfight as if it
were all there was to the man" (203). Moreover, Hamilton is apparently not the man he had always thought
himself to be. This new aspect of himself, more irratio-
nal than gallant, disturbs him even as it excites and im-
presses Roger—a fact that disturbs him all the more.

The closing scene of "Bicycles, Muscles, Cigarettes"
ranks among the most moving in *Will You Please Be
Quiet, Please?* Father and son acknowledge how this episode has simultaneously estranged them and made
them more intimate with one another. Just as the scope
of his son's reality has been enlarged for Hamilton, the
depths of the man Roger had always given the casual
designation of "Dad," a reliable yet unremarkable fixture in his world, have been suddenly revealed.

He moved to kiss his son, but the boy began
talking.
"Dad, was grandfather strong like you? When he
was your age, I mean, you know, and you—"
"And I was nine years old? Is that what you
mean? Yes, I guess he was," Hamilton said.
"Sometimes I can hardly remember him," the boy
said. "I don't want to forget him or anything, you
know? You know what I mean, Dad?"
When Hamilton did not answer at once, the boy
went on. "When you were young, was it like what it is
with you and me? Did you love him more than me?
Or just the same?" (204).

WILL YOU PLEASE BE QUIET, PLEASE?

Ironically, whereas Hamilton is concerned that he is a prisoner of a heritage (the latest in the family line of brutes and smokers, as it were), Roger is appeased by the possibility of continuity; he probes for evidence of himself in the family history as though it were a kind of guarantee. As the Hamilton past and his own future stretch out before him, the boy wants to arrest time, to stabilize and preserve this moment of intimacy:

"Dad? You'll think I'm pretty crazy, but I wish I'd known you when you were little. I mean, about as old as I am right now. I don't know how to say it, but I'm lonesome about it. It's like—it's like I miss you already if I think about it now. That's pretty crazy, isn't it? Anyway, please leave the door open" (205).

For once, not knowing "how to say it" does not invalidate experience. Hamilton's decision to close the door halfway symbolizes a compromise between the innocence he desires for his son and the confusing adult realm from which he cannot always protect him. But communication has been established and the door between them remains open. Hamilton's compassion leavens the painful process of growing up; it also confers upon this father an exalted status in Carver's world.

In "What Is It?" Leo and Toni have no such shared feeling to call upon in a financial crisis that unveils all manner of resentment and selfishness. Here it is the wife who is sent out on a mission to sell their old convertible before the storm of creditors arrives. While she is polished and composed—an experienced saleswoman, she originally met Leo when she sold him children's encyclopedias even though he did not have any kids—her husband is fretful, annoying. As the moment of truth approaches, the breach between them becomes increasingly clear:

"You look fine," he says. "You look great. I'd buy a car from you anytime."

"But you don't have any money," she says, peering into the mirror. She pats her hair, frowns. "And your credit's lousy. You're nothing," she says. "Teasing," she says and looks at him in the mirror (207).

As she leaves, Leo remembers last winter's affair; Ernest Williams, the neighbor from across the street who had seen him bring that woman into the house, seems to glower at him like a personal nemesis. Perhaps a successful sale of the car will redeem him, Leo thinks, and give the marriage a second chance.

But the hours pass, and Leo succumbs to anxiety. When he was only a child, he had learned that "bankruptcy" was no exotic term reserved for huge companies and mythic executives but an immediate, indiscriminate scourge. He tries to reconstruct his demise to exonerate himself for his current condition, but he begins to feel suicidal. And why is it taking his wife so long to contact him?

WILL YOU PLEASE BE QUIET, PLEASE?

When she finally calls—she is out for dinner and drinks with the prospective buyer—Leo projects his own untrustworthiness on her. Not until dawn does she get home with the news that she has gotten more than double what they had expected for the car. But what else has she "sold"? He strips her for evidence of her treachery; with disdainful fury she calls him "Bankrupt" and taunts him to strike her. Her evening's companion drives up, but Leo, bankrupt indeed, is not equal to the task of a confrontation; he has waived his rights to righteous indignation. The man quizzes Leo briefly about the mileage on the car, asking for an honest answer "between friends," and leaves. The sale has been made, but it will salvage nothing. Leo returns to the bedroom. He absently traces his wife's naked body with his fingers and recollects the day he had awakened to the gleaming new car in the driveway: both examples of squandered promise.

"Signals" refers not only to the tokens of social distinction Wayne and Caroline are so sensitive to at an elegant French restaurant, but also to the evidence of seismic disturbance in their relationship. An expensive dinner at Aldo's was intended to be the inauguration of that phantom second chance that Leo and Toni had blown in the previous story. However, Wayne and Caroline are so self-conscious, so intensely eager about noting the "classy" appointments that set this restaurant apart (including Aldo's own celebrity connections), that they merely embarrass themselves. Under more pleasant circumstances their gaucheries would be excusable, but because such dire emphasis has been placed on this evening, every vulgarity (comparing their champagne to Lancer's, fingering the relish tray, quarreling over how to hold the menu to achieve the best effect) stabs deeply.

Inevitably their marital aggravations leach into their conversation. When they have difficulty with the new waiter who cannot speak much English, they act gracelessly and assume that they have been deliberately assigned an incompetent. The desperate bid for a "good time" has failed. Aldo himself meets them as they leave, offering Caroline a rose and kissing her hand; however, Wayne dismisses this demonstration as artificial and decides to discredit the place by suggesting that Aldo probably never knew Lana Turner after all. If he cannot save face, he will not go down alone.

"Will You Please Be Quiet, Please?" is the volume's most ambitious story; in a sense it is also its most forgiving.[20] The somewhat Polonian advice of his father about the virtues of enterprise in the face of hardship ushers Ralph Wyman into his adult life. He drifts through his early college career, during which time he frequents the local bar more regularly than the library, until he meets Dr. Maxwell, a teacher whose stylish self-possession inspires him. Ralph fixes on the teaching profession, applies himself to his studies, and encounters and marries Marian, who is also preparing to become a teacher.

The fairy-tale biography begins to unravel for Ralph during their honeymoon in Guadalajara, where he "was secretly appalled by the squalor and open lust he saw and was anxious to return to the safety of California" (227). When he observes his wife leaning provocatively over the balustrade of their *casita*, he intuits an essential difference between their natures, as though he were witnessing "an intensely dramatic moment" from a film "into which Marian could be fitted but he could not" (227). Her unselfconscious demonstration of sensuality suggests the rupture to come.

This disparity between Ralph's constriction and Marian's receptivity had been heralded by Carver's introductions to these respective characters: Ralph had taken college courses in literature and philosophy and sensed he was "on the brink of some kind of huge discovery about himself," but none materialized (225); Marian, on the other hand, was depicted as having large eyes that "seemed to take in everything at a glance" (226). Whereas he takes a position at his old high school, she finds a job teaching at a junior college at the edge of town. From the start, Marian is innately available to a superior breadth of experience.

Sexual transgression epitomizes this. For years now Ralph has suspected his wife of having had sex with one of their dinner guests after a party they had hosted. As it happens, the subject of Ralph's paranoia comes up with the kids asleep, Marian ironing, and Ralph feeling happy and at peace. Whether it is because she needs to confess or because she feels secure enough at this moment to let Ralph in on her bemusement, Marian is the one who brings up that night. Ralph presses her for information, first with forced nonchalance, then with urgency, until the conversation turns into a full-scale interrogation. Marian confirms his apprehensions—"It was an impulse, that's all I can say. It was the *wrong* impulse"—and Ralph has a revelation, but one that discloses how benighted he has been: " 'Christ! The word leaped out of him. 'But you've always been that way, Marian!' And he knew at once that he had uttered a new and profound truth" (233). Before him once again is that strange, disconcerting woman whom he had watched on the balcony.

Like Lee Waite in "Sixty Acres," Ralph yearns for the refuge of an impregnable silence, even if it is only "the clenched politeness that masks the impulse to shout, 'Shut up!' " that the title of the story indicates.[21] As Marian recounts the episode detail by detail, Ralph grows angry, nauseous, frantic—and perversely, impossibly, sexually tantalized in a way that recalls the bizarre transaction between the husband who spies on his wife in "The Idea." Marian pleads for forgiveness, both for the act itself and, just as importantly, for having made him bear the terrible burden of knowing about it, but there can be no "unsaying" it.

Ralph's nighttown adventures resuscitate Jackson, the long-suppressed alter ego whose name Ralph had originally borrowed from the owner of the bar he had frequented during his dissolute days in college. Jackson is a personality that could conceivably even the score with Marian. Under the spell of his distress reality has been translated and the placid veneer of his town has

WILL YOU PLEASE BE QUIET, PLEASE?

been stripped away. The most ordinary occurrences—the way a woman tosses her hair as she gets into a car, for example—seem incredible, terrifying, and Ralph is convinced that "there was a great evil pushing at the world" that "only needed a little slipway, a little opening" to overwhelm him (239).

Wandering through alien, haunted streets, he comes upon Jim's Oyster House, whose comical sign (a man half-swallowed in a massive shell) parodies his feeling of suffocation. Once inside he eavesdrops on vulgar conversations, drinks too much, urinates on his hands, studies obscene graffiti. The squalor tightens about him, but his need for sympathetic inclusion overcomes his disgust. He joins a card game in the back room where he announces himself to be Jackson. Composed a bit by the masculine fellowship, Ralph confesses Marian's betrayal. He loses money, but the effect seems to be less ignominious than purgative. When he finally leaves the place, he envisions how handsomely Dr. Maxwell would have handled such a calamity as contrasted with his own destitution. The dark night of the soul concludes with Ralph's being arbitrarily beaten up by a black man in a bizarre reversal of Ralph's imagined punishment of his errant wife.

Ralph returns home the next morning either as a victim of lost innocence or a beneficiary of renewed potential. His child asks what happened to his face, which is injured, of course, but perhaps has been metamorphosed. That Ralph cannot adopt an adequate or recognizable expression in the bathroom mirror suggests a clean slate, the elusive boon of a clean start other Carver characters have sought in vain. In the end Ralph turns away from the mirror and toward his wife, and this sets him apart from the swarm of self-interred protagonists who have preceded him in *Will You Please Be Quiet, Please?* Although the last scene may be intellectually unsatisfying, and is certainly not the result of a conscious, intrepid choice on Ralph's part, it is dynamic and displays an availability to life:

> He tensed at her fingers, and then he let go a little. It was easier to let go a little. Her hand moved over his hip and over his stomach and she was pressing her body over his now and moving over him and back and forth over him. He held himself, he later considered, as long as he could. And then he turned to her. He turned and turned in what might have been a stupendous sleep, and he was still turning, marveling at the impossible changes he felt moving over him (249).

"Finding out" his wife has come to mean more than just unearthing her sin; it means discovering who she is. Similarly, Ralph has managed to acknowledge a side of himself that helps to complete him. It is not corruption he succumbs to, but a broadening that has enabled him to "unclench" and respond.

Carver does not pad his characters with adjectives or arm them with vocabularies against the world's iniquities. *Will You Please Be Quiet, Please?* does document the occasional lurid skirmish, but on the whole, things remain lukewarm; arid marriages and formulated phrases are the norm. Desires, doubts, and all manner of considerations flow sluggishly through the narrowest of verbal channels. Under these circumstances silence is usually a cover for insufficiency. Nevertheless, the conclusion of the title story—the closing paragraph of the book—intimates a state of acceptance in which silence does not necessarily represent defeat; for Ralph Wyman it accompanies a resumption of life. Admittedly, this does not offset the dominant tone of the volume, which is severe and unyielding. Not until the publication of *Cathedral* does this relatively optimistic mood appear with any regularity. But it is important not to neglect the moments in *Will You Please Be Quiet, Please?* that *surpass* language, specifically, the private marvels that befall Evan Hamilton and Ralph Wyman. They read like achievements and stand out in relief against the surrenders that typify Carver's early fiction.

Notes

1. Although some of the stories gathered together in *Furious Seasons* antedate stories that appear in *Will You Please Be Quiet, Please?* critics generally regard the latter as Carver's first collection. *Will You Please Be Quiet, Please?* was Carver's first book to be published by a major press, and its appearance triggered his rapid rise to prominence.

2. "Hills Like White Elephants," *The Short Stories of Ernest Hemingway* (New York: Scribner's, 1953) 227.

3. *Paterson* (New York: New Directions, 1963).

4. *The Minimal Self: Psychic Survival in Troubled Times* (New York: Norton, 1984) 15.

5. David Boxer and Cassandra Phillips, *"Will You Please Be Quiet, Please?* Voyeurism, Dissociation, and the Art of Raymond Carver," *Iowa Review* 10 (1979): 78–79.

6. Mona Simpson, interview, "The Art of Fiction LXXVI," *Paris Review* 25 (1983): 207.

7. "Fat," *Will You Please Be Quiet, Please?* (New York: McGraw-Hill, 1976) 2,4,6. Subsequent references to stories in this volume are noted parenthetically in the text.

8. "The Order of Insects," *In the Heart of the Heart of the Country* (New York: Harper, 1968) 167.

9. Martin Esslin, *Pinter: A Study of His Plays*, expanded ed. (New York: Norton, 1970) 40.

10. Boxer and Phillips 84.

11. Simpson, interview, 213–14.

12. "Conversation with the Supplicant," *The Penal Colony: Stories and Short Pieces*. trans. Willa and Edwin Muir (New York: Schocken, 1976) 14.

13. James Purdy, *Malcolm* (New York: Farrar, Strauss, 1959); John Barth, *The End of the Road* (Garden City, NY: Doubleday, 1967).

14. A profitable comparison could be made to William Gass's Fender, the protagonist of "Icicles," who is but one of the spiderlike characters in *In the Heart of the Heart of the Country*. He describes himself as "a man without a place to be, a place that's known, that has a name, is some way fixed; why that's like being alone at sea without a log to hang on—and the sharks at your toes. . . . Yes, he thought, I do not even occupy myself" (157). Carver, too, presents numerous characters who define themselves by what they lack.

15. e. e. cummings, introduction, *New Poems, Complete Poems: 1913-1962*, ed. George James Firmage (New York: Harcourt Brace, 1968) 461.

WILL YOU PLEASE BE QUIET, PLEASE?

16. Quoted in Arnold Bauer, *Rainer Maria Rilke* (New York: Ungar, 1972) 61.

17. Quoted in Bruce Weber, "Raymond Carver: A Chronicler of Blue-Collar Despair," *New York Times Magazine* 24 June 1984: 48.

18. Arthur Miller, *Death of a Salesman* (New York: Viking, 1949) 56.

19. "Harry's Death," *Fires* (Santa Barbara, CA: Capra, 1983) 140. Death obliterates him; the narrator cannot even locate his grave.

20. It is also among its most heralded. "Will You Please Be Quiet, Please?" won inclusion in *Best American Short Stories of 1967*, edited by Martha Foley. Three other stories in this volume were published in O. Henry Award Annual collections: "What Is It?" (1973), "Put Yourself in My Shoes" (1974), and "Are You a Doctor?" (1975).

21. Boxer and Phillips 87.

CHAPTER THREE

Furious Seasons

In his essay "Fires," Carver concedes similarities between his writing and Hemingway's, but he speaks in terms of admiration rather than influence.[1] Whatever the origin or character of this kinship, it is most apparent in the opening stories of *Furious Seasons*. Set among the working-class inhabitants of the Pacific Northwest, these stories display a terse surface and a simple respect for the marvels of nature that readily provoke the comparison to Hemingway's fiction. Apart from the title story, in which Carver makes surprising use of stream-of-consciousness techniques, the fictions in this collection are generally faithful to such conventions as narrative framing and definitive closure and thus represent a clear stylistic departure from so-called minimalist characteristics.

"Dummy" in particular recalls Hemingway's Nick Adams stories. There is the same splendid understatement instigated by the same simple events, as though the poetry inherent in the leap of fish or a drive by a pasture outdoes language so that only "My God," or "It was a sight to behold," or "Great to be alive" can be summoned in response. Carver clearly shares Hemingway's dedication to telling it cleanly:

The bass jump-jumped around the pond and every
time it came up out of the water it shook its head, and
we could hear the plug rattle. And then the bass
would take off on another run. In ten minutes I had
the fish on its side, a few feet from shore. It looked
enormous, six or seven pounds, maybe, and it lay on
its side, whipped, mouth open and gills working
slowly. My knees felt so weak I could hardly stand,
but I held the rod up, the line tight. Father waded out
over his shoes.[2]

"Dummy" is an initiation story for the narrator, who had been twelve at the time of the story's occurrence, for his father, and for the title character, who, deaf and dumb, had been given that name by the workers at the Cascade Lumber Company in Yakima, Washington, as a form of good-natured abuse. Like Singer's Gimpel the Fool, Dummy is an easy, perpetual victim of practical jokes and salacious gossip about the activities of his young wife. "For me," the narrator confesses, "Dummy's death signalled the end of my extraordinarily long childhood, sending me forth, ready or not, into the world of men—where defeat and death are more in the natural order of things" (9).

Ironically, it is Dummy's effort to enhance his life by stocking his pond with black bass that instigates his demise. Partly out of nostalgia for the bass fishing he had done back in Arkansas and Georgia as a boy and out of a desire to provide that essential rite of passage to his son, the narrator's father is delighted to think that, as Dummy's friend (or his one relatively sympathetic acquaintance), he will be able to share in this opportunity. However, witnessing the magical little bass fingerlings transforms Dummy; he grows strangely, anxiously protective of his treasure, and only after steady coercion admits the father and son to fish there.

At the outset the fishing expedition promises to be a success. Although a contrived event—the fish having been transplanted by mail to a private pond—it inspires awe and intimacy: "It's really great, isn't it, dad? I mean, I don't know, but everything's just fun we do, isn't it?" (17). But at the moment of triumph Dummy deliberately ruins the boy's catch. Perhaps Dummy has decided to exert a possessive influence over this portion of his life, his wife apparently having escaped his control; perhaps it is a matter of salvaging something he loves from contamination or injury. Whatever the case, the sanctuary is short-lived, for the heavy February rains flood his property. The father feels vindicated and sorry at the same time.

The end of "Dummy" seems inexorable and arrives almost immediately afterward. Dummy is found dead, a suicide (drowning), after having murdered his wife with a hammer. The narrator closes the frame of the story by noting that the tragedy also marked the decline of his father as well: "But it seemed to me life became more difficult for him after that, that he was never able to act happy and carefree any more" (26).

Retitled "The Third Thing That Killed My Father Off" in *What We Talk About When We Talk About Love*, this story is intended by its narrator to deflect attention from himself to his father, who is put forward as the story's real protagonist. Along with Pearl Harbor and the move to his grandfather's farm, two earlier "killing" events, Dummy is a factor in his *father's* story. Nevertheless, the brutal shattering of innocent pleasures, the incursion of life's ugliness, consumes the narrator as well and abruptly climaxes the special innocence that had characterized the father-son relationship. Revealing that he is as old now as his father had been during the incident he has related, the narrator has grown almost ruthlessly stoic about life. The sexual betrayals of Dummy's wife, the sight of an arm of Dummy's bloated corpse emerging from the water, the awareness of his father's fright, and "the misfortune that dogged our family in the coming years" have combined to steel the narrator against nostalgia or hope. Now he claims to be beyond impressionability, having "lived a while in the world—been around some, as they say—I know it now for what it was, that arm. Simply, the arm of a drowned man. I have seen others" (26). Something of the same jaded, resentful, powerless tone of his father toward the floods he could do nothing about is also detectable here. The world toughens or destroys people; it toughens *and* destroys them. Pleasures are fleeting and insights into the way of the world merely underline our helplessness before it. "Dummy" clarifies the irresistible fact of defeat. The story represents a momentary indulgence of personal despair over the human condition.

"Distance" also employs the frame technique that stabilizes the reader's perspective on the story. Like "Dummy," "Distance" is a ritual effort of repair in which the cunning art of memory proves serviceable to emotional needs. A young woman visiting her father in Milan urges him to tell the familiar story of their family life when she was a baby. The father relates the third-person "fable" of two teen-age parents living in a small apartment under a dentist's office. "These two kids, as I've told you, were very much in love. On top of this they had great ambitions and they were wild dreamers. They were always talking about the things they were going to do and the places they were going to go" (28). However, as in the previous story, the "good old days" are a treacherous legacy whose primary effect is to highlight the failure to sustain the optimistic vision of their future.

The first tremors are observed when the young father chooses to go hunting with Carl Sutherland, who had been a friend of his own dead father. What fishing was supposed to provide in "Dummy," hunting promises in "Distance": an opportunity to cement relationships and values. But the occasion sours because he deserts during the baby's mysterious crying episode. Despite the growing desperation of his wife, who cannot quell the persistent crying, he leaves the apartment. On the way to meet Carl he envies the "bright distance" of the stars (34), for they maintain a privileged distance from the tension, the noise, and the guilt that he wants to escape.

When the men meet, he relates the family crisis to Carl, who then plays down the importance and appeal of the hunt, thereby giving his companion an opportunity to bow out of the adventure gracefully.[3] He returns home to find the baby asleep and his wife eager to erase the argument. They laugh together over an overturned breakfast plate and gratefully forgive one another for the day's difficulties. The story-within-the-story concludes with an almost manufactured ease and a renewed commitment never to fight again.

The story completes its frame, returning over the distance of years and regrets to the grown daughter's desire to learn what happened later. That the father appears to reside alone now in Milan suggests that the composure he and his wife had achieved and had promised to adhere to was transitory. "Things change, he says. Kids grow up. I don't know what happened. But things do change and without your realizing it or wanting them to" (36).

In the story he related, the central metaphor emerged from a discussion with his wife of how geese mate for life; shooting one does not free the mate to "marry" another, but instead consigns the goose to solitude within the flock. Whereas his wife mourned the "sad fate" of geese and questioned how one could hunt them with such knowledge, the husband is dismissive, saying that he does not think about it when he hunts.

Although he appreciates the wonder of geese, he loves hunting them, too: "But there are all kinds of contradictions in life. You can't think about all the contradictions" (31). Not only does this discussion intimate a kind of distance between the two of them, it also becomes poignantly ironic when, mateless himself and despite relationships with other women, the father is also condemned to loneliness. The story of the geese had clearly been designed to serve as an object lesson, a symbolic confirmation of love's permanence to aid the young couple through difficult times; unfortunately, like the story that the father shares with his daughter, its final effect is to emphasize the inability to live up to such vows.

Thus, he has come a great distance after all from the wistful dreams of long ago.[4] His grown daughter has inherited his penchant for returning to the innocent time before the unnamed fractures in their lives had occurred. Even though she is described as "a survivor from top to bottom" in the version of "Distance" that appears in *What We Talk About When We Talk About Love* (a character note that recalls the narrator's approval of his own toughness of spirit in "Dummy"), there is no reason to expect that she will prove more resilient in the face of *her* fate. "Distance" closes with a communion of tears and laughter between father and daughter, "while outside everything froze, for a while anyway" (36).[5] Their solidarity, represented by their mutual participation in the family fiction, entrusts the fate of the family to the one context that, they hope, resists violation—an arrested moment in a three-room apartment when a loving embrace could seem both a solace and a guarantee.

The overriding question in *Furious Seasons*, then, is how much reality human relationships can tolerate. If wisdom is only hard on people, it must be treated as pernicious. In recollecting one of the most difficult periods of his own life, Carver complains that growth of understanding may be hostile if understanding merely provides a clearer sense of one's predicament:

Things would change some, but they were never really going to get better. I understood this, but could I live with it? At that moment I saw accommodations would have to be made. The sights would have to be lowered. I'd had, I realized later, an insight. But so what? What are insights? They don't help any. They just make things harder.[6]

In "The Lie" the husband who interrogates his wife about some infidelity he had been informed of feels victimized by his own accusation, for he cannot withstand the repercussions of the truth he may uncover:

I was uncomfortable. I stood there in my slippers opening and closing my hands, feeling a little ridiculous and on display in spite of the circumstances. I'm not cut out to play the inquisitor. I wish now it had never reached my ears, that everything could have been as before (37).

If his wife derogates the informing friend for rumor-mongering, he himself resents her for conferring upon him the responsibility to follow through. But just as he manages to convince himself that the informant was the liar, his wife confesses her own lie. Quickly, by reflex, he takes refuge in sexual consolation and infantile oblivion:

"Come up here, dumpling. Did it really believe that nasty lady, that nasty lie? Here, put your head on mommy's breast. That's it. Now close your eyes. There. How could it believe such a thing? I'm disappointed in you. Really, you know me better than that. Lying is just a sport for some people" (40).

This is reminiscent of the conclusion of John Osborne's *Look Back in Anger*, in which the beleaguered couple retire into a "fuzzy-brained" game of bears and squirrels, or of Edward Albee's *Who's Afraid of Virginia Woolf?* in which George and Martha tend to their bruises after a long night's trial by exposure. The husband in "The Lie" had been reading Tolstoy, a writer who is renowned for his stalwart defense of art as an instrument of morality and truth. But the "art" practiced by this couple is their mutual evasion of the consequences of falsity. Indeed, the nature of truth that they opt for is closer to what they witnessed in the film *Blow-Up*, in which the distinction between truth and illusion is ambiguous and subjective, and hence manipulatable. Tolstoy is trumped by emotional priorities; he is rendered harmless by being appropriated into the odd little game they play to comfort themselves (she calls her troubled husband "my little muzhik" and "little Pasha"). Lies are the inevitable premium they pay to survive together as hostages of their secrets.

The barrier that divides Claire and Stuart in "So Much Water So Close to Home" is fortified by his refusal, or inability, to recognize its profundity: "Something has come between us though he would like to believe otherwise" (41). On a camping trip Stuart and three friends come across a dead girl (a victim of rape and murder, it turns out) floating in the river. Rather than attend to her immediately, which would delay their vacation, they decide to leave her in the water and just anchor her to a tree until they complete two days of fishing, drinking, and card playing. Only then do they call the sheriff to describe their "grisly find." The fact that he could be so deliberately indifferent leads his wife to the brink of a nervous breakdown, which is intensified by his astonishing incomprehension. She hates him for his repeated self-justifications (since the girl was already dead, he did not really fail to help her), but she also pities him for the measliness of his efforts to defend himself against her accusations.

Most disturbing, however, is the sudden sense of estrangement she feels from him: "He puts his heavy arms around me and rubbed his hands up and down my back, the same hands he'd left with two days before, I thought" (44). A similar moment of arrest occurs between the husband and wife in Robert Frost's "Home Burial" as they come to realize the true extent of their alienation from one another. Because she perceives his having buried their dead child as proof of his insensitivity—he is able to dig their child's grave, "making the gravel leap and leap in the air"—a shadow encloses the whole of their relationship, past and future: "I thought, Who is that man? I didn't know you."[7] The frustrations of the husband who cannot please his wife with either explanation or silence is just as instructive. Driven to distraction by his wife's willful inconsolability, he considers how it might be preferable to effect a kind of treaty between them according to which especially troublesome subjects would not be broached; however, he recognizes that such agreements signify the doom of intimacy: "Two that don't love can't live together without them, / But two that do can't live together with them."[8]

In "So Much Water So Close to Home," Stuart oscillates between sexual advances (significantly, he had had sex with his wife *before* relating the story of the dead girl) and denial of wrongdoing, whose ferocity suggests his underlying shame. As for Claire, she adopts the judgmental policy of her mother-in-law, by whom she herself has always felt judged, and thereby extends the circuitry of guilt that characterizes their family. Like the woman in "The Lie," she longs to reverse the process of experience, to deinitiate herself; the story's title is her complaint that Stuart need not have gone so far off to fish. She blames him for condemning them to confront one another so terribly, for shrinking before her eyes. "I could laugh in his face. I could weep" (48).

As Claire becomes more erratic, she begins to notice her husband's hairy legs, his vulgar manners; she slaps him and regrets the irrelevancy, the craziness of it. She is haunted by a vision of herself floating face down in the water. All the while she both wishes for a return to routine and fears that this is precisely what is in store for her, for the crisis has disqualified their marriage:

> Two things are certain: 1) people no longer care what happens to other people, and 2) nothing makes any real difference any longer. Look at what has happened. Yet nothing will change for Stuart and me. Really change. We will grow older, both of us, you can see it in our faces already, in the bathroom mirror, for instance, mornings when we use the bathroom at the same time. And certain things around us will change, become easier or harder, one thing or the other, but nothing will ever really be any different. I believe that. We have made our decisions, our lives have been set in motion, and they will go on and on until they stop. But if that is true, what then? I mean, what if you believe that, but you keep it covered up, until one day something happens that should change something, but then you see nothing is going to change after all. What then? (49).

These concerns and recriminations remain nebulous and unspoken. Claire feebly objects to having been sentenced to a fate that she did not make.

They grasp at reestablishing their routines and reacquainting themselves with one another—could there ever have been intimacy between us? she wonders. But when her son asks Claire about the event, or when she thinks of the girl she knew at school who had been raped, or when she puzzles over the seductive forays of her own husband, her anxiety is reignited. Outraged over having to cope with her, Stuart flaunts his obscure injuries before her; the continual interest in the crime on television and in the newspapers seems like a conspiracy of the media to keep their private wounds open. Claire begins to sleep alone; Stuart musters little more than vague pleas or vague threats.

Out of either morbid curiosity or a need to face her obsession immediately, Claire decides to go to the girl's funeral. However, because her confidence in her marriage, as well as in the self she had always identified through her marriage, has deteriorated, she is not only an intruder but an unreliable witness. Even her brief note to her son telling him she will be home later and to stay close to the house strikes her as odd, foreign: "As I am writing the note I realize I don't know whether *back yard* is one word or two. I have never considered it before" (55). She travels the 117-mile trip in a daze, feeling empty and unjustifiable. A truck approaches in the next lane, and her imagination fills with corpses and victims of rape. She pulls over and the trucker approaches, but her interpretive powers are so impaired that she cannot discern his motives. Is he really concerned about her welfare? Is he staring at her breasts and legs? " 'I want

to smother.' I say. 'I am smothering, can't you see?' "
(57). At the funeral she tries vainly to come to terms
with an inexplicable sense of urgency to pay back her
husband's indefensible failure or to find for herself a
defensible place in the grief of strangers: "There is a
connection to be made of these things, these events,
these faces, if I can find it. My head aches with the
effort to find it" (58).

Back home, she stammers something about being
afraid; Stuart offers his clumsy commiseration, fingers
the buttons on her jacket and blouse. The cycle of mis-
understanding and injury continues: he rages at her for
fighting against his sexual insistence; he sends flowers
and a fumbling apology. But wasn't the delivery boy
staring at her suggestively, standing as though daring
her to touch him? One night Stuart bursts the lock on
her door, just to show that he can, just to reinforce his
possession, and in her mind is replayed the rape of an
unknown girl. "It doesn't matter, Stuart. Really, I tell
you it doesn't matter one way or the other" (61), she
tells him on the phone, referring to his mother's impending visit, or to his angry trespasses, or to the use-
lessness of anything he might try to do. The story ends
with the relationship on this precipice.

The formal resolution that marks "Dummy" and
"Distance" is absent in "So Much Water So Close to
Home." But a full appreciation of this story requires that
its closing in *Furious Seasons* be contrasted with the revised ending Carver employs in the later version of the
story that appears in *What We Talk About When We Talk*

UNDERSTANDING RAYMOND CARVER

About Love, in which the story is considerably trimmed. Stuart is now less pleading; responses between husband and wife are automatic; and the effect of these abbreviations is to intensify the sense of the unavoidability of the decline of the marriage. Most important, however, is that whereas the earlier version concludes with a final verification of separation, for the specter of the dead girl still looms and overwhelms his protestations of love and innocence, the later version ends with Claire's willful abandonment to his initial sexual advances:

> "First things first," he says.
> He says something else. But I don't need to listen. I can't hear a thing with so much water going.
> "That's right," I say, finishing the buttons myself. "Before Dean comes. Hurry."[9]

In the later version Claire returns from the funeral anxious to restore her commitment to life. Nevertheless, the future of the marriage is no more inspiring despite the reimagined ending of the story. Anxiety, not forgiveness or compassion, motivates her now. The sound of water is a welcome oblivion, a shrinking from insight, and the reader is reminded of the last lines of "Sixty Acres": "He shut his eyes and brought his hands against his ears to steady himself. And then he thought to cup his palms, so that there would come that roaring, like the wind howling up from a seashell."[10] Whether or not, depending on which version of "So Much Water"

FURIOUS SEASONS

one reads, Claire is granted a short reprieve from consciousness, there will still be that contaminant, that
dead girl's ghost, that will discredit her pleasures and
scuttle her dreams.

After the unique circumstances of "So Much Water
So Close to Home," the history of an extramarital affair
seems rather mundane; but of course what is ordinary
in the abstract is often profoundly significant when one
is directly implicated. Like "Dummy," "The Fling" is a
son's story of, or for, his father, and again the narrative
act is revealed as being simultaneously an attempt to
achieve distance and an acceptance of involvement. The
son's retelling of his father's confession of the adultery
that precipitated his divorce is framed by the son's efforts to sort out filial duties and proprieties. He is irri-
tated by the burden of having to serve as a sounding
board for his father: there is something tragic, even un-
natural, about a child's having to shoulder his parent's
weaknesses. The pressure to exonerate his father sparks
his violent disapproval:

For a moment he seemed utterly contemptible to me,
and I had to look away. I knew I was being silly, that
I'd be gone in another hour, but it was all I could do
to keep from telling him then what I thought of his
dirty little affair, and what it had done to my mother
(71).

However, this reaction has less to do with sympathy for
his mother or moral outrage than with his consternation

at finding his father so small, so besieged, and just his size.

The details of the affair are as unremarkable, if not as cheap or tawdry, as the title of the story suggests (at least, until it is discovered that his father had had to leap through the front room window to avoid her husband, who subsequently died from puncturing himself repeatedly with a paring knife). Were it not for the fact that it was his father, the events would have been altogether ludicrous. Ultimately, "The Fling" reveals itself to be a prolonged rationalization by the narrator for his failure to respond sufficiently to the naked neediness of his father:

> He started to say something else, but shook his head. Then he leaned forward slightly across the table, lips parted still, trying to find my eyes. He wanted something. He was trying to involve me in it someway, all right, but it was more than that, he wanted something else. An answer, maybe, when there were no answers. Maybe a simple gesture on my part, a touch on the arm, perhaps. Maybe that would have been enough (76).

Whatever boon the father is after, his son can only muster a fumbling, customary good-bye. As in Bellow's *Seize the Day*, the perpetual bargaining for approval and sympathy between father and son is limited by strict rules of access. They stalk one another for understanding.

FURIOUS SEASONS

After that last meeting the son "imitates" his father's failure in marriage. "He caused me—*forced* might be the better word—to peer into my own abyss" (63), but it did not enable him to avoid disaster in his own relationship. In a sense the narrator has felt hemmed in instead of enlarged by the lesson of his father. Telling "The Fling" has not explained his father to him nor excused him for his inaction; just as the wronged husband who was driven to suicide would remain on his father's conscience, the image of his confused father being hurriedly packed into a cab stays with him. "But, tell me, after all, what could he expect from someone like me?" he asks (78). Love and guilt—the common, pathetic concoctions of the heart.

In "Pastoral," as in "Nobody Said Anything" in *Will You Please Be Quiet, Please?* Carver shows how even the abiding comforts of nature can be tainted by the enmities that ruin relationships. Whether it is his wife's decision not to accompany Mr. Harold to the cabin that corrupts the place for him now, or whether its dilapidation since their last visit together three years earlier intensifies his awareness of his problems with Frances, what once seemed edenic is now revealed as a tacky approximation of the frontier, complete with Indian souvenirs. The eager friendliness of the proprietors seems suspicious, tinny; he discovers that the fishermen have been crowded out by boisterous deer hunters; his lodgings cramp him, and he cannot get comfortable or organized. His anger at his absent wife, whom he suspects has somehow sabotaged this refuge, begins to swell.

Even when he leaves the cabin to go fishing the next day, the hope of rekindling the triumphs and satisfactions of the past strays into desperate confusion and portends his coming humiliation. Holding his rod like a lance, he remembers pretending as a boy that he was

in the lists coming down on his opponent. The jays at the crowded edge of the woods screaming for him. Then, when it was over, he would sing something as loud as he could. Yell defiance until his chest hurt, at the hawks that circled and circled over the meadow. The sun and the lace sky, and the back lake with the lean-to. The water was clear and green; you could see fifteen, twenty feet down to where it shelved off. Behind the trees he could hear the fall of the river. The trail was gone and just before he started down the bank to the river, he stepped into a snow drift up over his knees and panicked, clawing up handfuls of snow and vines to get out (86).

He recalls this feeling of disequilibrium when he enters the river to his waist to begin fishing. The spatter of gunshots inhibits his efforts to recapture the old excitement; unsettled, a little nauseous, he thinks he has chosen the wrong place in the river. He sees a wounded deer and curses the hunters for their incursion. They arrive on the bank—ungainly, obscene boys, who take vicious pleasure in brandishing their guns at him. They taunt him with stones, which they hurl so that they

splash around him. "You didn't want to fish here anyway, did you?" one of them cries. "I could've got you,
but I didn't. Now you see that deer, remember how
lucky you was. Hear?" (90).

Harold escapes to the woods but loses his rod (the
lance of his daydreams and the emblem of his former
prowess) in doing so.

Somehow he had missed it and it was gone.
Something heroic. He didn't know what he was going
to do. He couldn't very well go home. Slow, thick
flakes sifted down through the freezing air, sticking on
his coat collar, melting cold and wet against his face.
He stared at the wordless, distorted things around
him (91).

Swarmed over by his losses, he ends in full retreat.[11]

In under five hundred words "Mine" updates the
Bible tale of the contest between two women over an
infant, but Carver provides no Solomon to arbitrate between his two battling, embattled parents. Leaving her,
the husband fastens on the baby as a validation of his
past and foundation for his future; defying him, the
wife clings ferociously for the same reason. The baby is
almost literally pulled apart by their absolute selfishness; the baby is an "issue" to be resolved, a point of
contention, an object to be possessed. Surrendering
custody would be a symbolic admission of blame that
neither parent can afford to shoulder. "Mine" is a minor
piece, but it concisely renders a major theme of the vol-

ume: to what destructive lengths will people go to justify themselves to themselves?

The title story compels an evaluation of the squalid episodes that pervade *Furious Seasons* against the vastness of time and nature, which, though it reduces all human striving to pettiness, perhaps opens even the most outrageous actions to the reader's sympathy. Unusual among Carver's stories for its disruption of linear progression, its conflation of dream and reality, and a surprising lushness of style, "Furious Seasons" exhibits the traumatic consequences for Lew Farrell of his sister's pregnancy and death, both of which he seems to have caused. Whether or not Farrell is guilty of incest and murder is obscured by his subjective meanderings and lapses of focus; he shifts back and forth between robotlike desensitization and surreal images of suffocation and violence. To complicate matters further, words themselves seem to him untrustworthy and alien, reminding one of Claire's suspicion of the divorce between language and sense in "So Much Water So Close to Home": "The words are dry, hurrying like old leaves into the dark corners of the room and Farrell feels at the same instant the words are out that the question has already been asked by someone else, a long time ago" (95). Finally, there are numerous descriptions of the portentous qualities of the night churning with rain and nightmare. On such a night the mind roams freely into memory, fantasy, and apprehension without distinguishing among them. World crises encountered in *National Geographic*, a vision of his father's workmanlike

FURIOUS SEASONS

evisceration of a sheep, a living tableau of his sister naked before him—a host of grotesque and strangely accu-
satory images swarm through Farrell's consciousness.

Meanwhile, the action of the story ventures into familiar Carver territory as Farrell goes hunting for geese
with his friend Frank. But Farrell's turbulent inner
"weather" crowds out the physical realities around
him. Crouching alone in a blind, he slips into reveries
about previous expeditions, or he dimly recollects eating apples with his sister as though betokening their
sin. To borrow a phrase from Kurt Vonnegut regarding
Billy Pilgrim in *Slaughterhouse-Five*, Farrell comes "un-
stuck in time." Either time has stopped cold in this alien
rainworld, like the broken clock on Frank's dashboard
or the indecipherable glow from Farrell's bedroom
clock, or time's infinite sweep has closed in upon him
all at once:

A wet breeze off the river blew against his face. The
sides of the low bluffs overlooking the river down
below were deeply grooved and cut back into the rock,
leaving table-like projections jutting out, marking the
high water lines for thousands of years past. Piles of
naked white logs and countless pieces of driftwood lay
jammed onto the ledge like cairns of bones dragged
up onto the cliffs by some giant bird (104).

He drops off to sleep and awakens to a malevolent fog.
Panicking, Farrell forgets his kill and rushes out to find
Frank, who tries to console him about what he assumes

are the normal disturbances of his home life. When they find a police car waiting at Farrell's house upon their return, Frank jokes about Farrell's getting caught for hunting without a license. He drops Farrell off to fend for himself against the welter of forces that have conspired against him from the start: "Farrell holding onto the tail fin, swaying a little, with the fine impenetrable rain coming down around him. The gutter water rushed over his feet, swirled frothing into a great whirlpool at the drain on the corner and rushed down to the center of the earth" (110).

In "Furious Seasons" Carver not only experiments formally, he expands the context of crisis beyond the domestic boundaries that generally hold throughout the rest of the collection. But the furies that victimize his characters are always personally and privately endured. "The pure products of America / go crazy" begins Williams's poem "To Elsie"[12]; *Furious Seasons* is deeply attuned to what are conventionally offered as the saving resources of American life: invigorating activities that bring the reader close to nature. Tragically, however, Carver's characters are too haunted, too disheartened, or too late to benefit. Yearnings and failures they cannot voice hold them hostage.

Notes

1. "On Writing," *Fires: Essays, Poems, Stories* (Santa Barbara: Capra, 1983) 13.

2. "Dummy," *Furious Seasons* (Santa Barbara, CA: Capra, 1977) 21. Subsequent page references to stories in this volume are noted parenthetically in the text.

3. In two later versions of this story he never reaches Carl at all. The pull of regret and duty is strong enough to hold him there by itself.

4. In *What We Talk About When We Talk About Love* the story is retitled "Everything Stuck to Him," which distinctly implies that "distance" is not salvation but only a confirmation of his "sad fate."

5. The revised version of the concluding line of the story as it appears in *What We Talk About When We Talk About Love* stresses the desired function of the father's story as a stay against his own confusion: "They had leaned on each other and laughed until the tears had come, while everything else—the cold, and where he'd go in it—was outside, for a while anyway." "Everything Stuck to Him," *What We Talk About When We Talk About Love* (New York: Knopf, 1981) 135.

6. "Fires," *Fires* 24.

7. "Home Burial," *Complete Poems of Robert Frost* (New York: Holt, Rinehart, 1958) 71.

8. "Home Burial" 70–71.

9. "So Much Water So Close to Home", *What We Talk About When We Talk About Love* 88.

10. "Sixty Acres," *Will You Please Be Quiet, Please?* (New York: McGraw-Hill, 1976) 74.

11. The version of "Pastoral" that appears in *Fires* as "The Cabin" concludes with his returning to his cabin to try to warm himself again before the fire: "He began to think of home, of getting back there before dark" (138). But here, too, going home does not represent his positive determination to rebuild a relationship; it signals only one more retreat.

12. "To Elsie," *The William Carlos Williams Reader*, ed. M. L. Rosenthal (New York: New Directions, 1966) 17.

CHAPTER FOUR

What We Talk About When We Talk About Love

Frustrations burn like scraped nerves throughout Carver's third collection. Every story documents the ducks and feints of couples who prefer the static of "human noise" to the rigors of more substantial contact. Carver continues to write about America's written-off—people who cannot communicate and bemoan that impairment constantly. What they talk about when they talk about love is usually anything but. As in the preceding collections Carver's characters settle for abbreviations; because the ties that bind them together are so tenuous, they are forever making long stories short.

What We Talk About When We Talk About Love is Carver at his most astringent. The prose style displays the subtle ravages it recounts and runs almost to formula: gelid, skeletal sentences, stifled descriptions, pedestrian diction, and a narrative voice that "seems to come from the furniture."[1] Carver has received regular congratulations for the economy of his language, but "economy," with its connotations of clarity, effectiveness, and control, hardly applies to the shapeless complaints of the characters themselves, whose verbal supply seldom matches the demands of true intimacy. The myth of snugness, of at-homeness, erodes in the sinister air of these fictions.

Carver admits that his strictly rationed narrative "moves" originate from an intentional working through of a particular aesthetic.[2] Further evidence of his deliberation, perhaps, is the fact that five of the seventeen stories in this volume are slightly revised versions of stories from *Furious Seasons*.[3] The first of the new stories, "Why Don't You Dance?" opens with the image of a man's furniture and appliances all arranged and operating in his front yard.[4] The inversion of his home imitates the reversal of his fortunes, which, although they are never specifically revealed, probably have to do with a broken marriage. This bizarre personal inventory appears to be the self's going-out-of-business sale, a systematic exteriorization of old wounds: "He had run an extension cord on out there and everything was connected. Things worked, no different from how it was when they were inside."[5] Throughout the story the man maintains the regulated bemusement that is the stage beyond despair. *His* story has already ended, and perhaps his deliberate disorientation of his household is his attempt to orient himself to the rules that now govern his life.

Turning his inside out, as it were, renders him vulnerable to the unabashed voyeurism that has always pervaded Carver's suburbs. When he leaves for the market, a young couple happens by and, assuming this must be a yard sale, blithely begin to invade the premises, trying out the television, the blender, and the bed in a rehearsal of the postures and affections they hope to suit to these items. Since they are in the process of furnishing their own apartment, their predatory instincts are particularly sharp; the girl's intuition that here is a man who can be successfully haggled with is more than confirmed upon his return, as the man proceeds to place ridiculously low prices on his belongings. Perhaps he is grateful for their occupation of the "camp" because it provides a chance to disburden himself of the cloying connections to his past; on the other hand, this wholesale surrender may be his way of undervaluing himself out of existence.

All the while, domestic commonplaces are made enigmatic by their displacement and exposure to the neighborhood. Water from the outdoor spigot dilutes their drinks as they watch television on the lawn, and in this confused context every motive is inscrutable: "In the lamplight, there was something about their faces. It was nice or it was nasty. There was no telling" (7–8). Will the young couple contract the same disease from the sofa he perched upon, his restless bed? As they relax into their future accommodations, the man suggests they test out his phonograph. The old records play, and as the boy writes out a comprehensive check, the man enjoins them to dance. Soon all three are moving languidly to music the buyers cannot identify. Under the influence of liquor and nostalgia, a brief sexual pulse arises:

"Those people over there, they're watching," she said.

"It's okay," the man said. "It's my place," he said.

"Let them watch," the girl said.

"That's right," the man said. "They thought they'd seen everything over here. But they haven't seen this, have they?" he said.

He felt her breath on his neck.

"I hope you like your bed," he said (9).

This is pride's last stand. But what has been exchanged in this middle-class allegory? To him, there is "no telling" what their faces hold; to them, the strange man "must be desperate or something" (9). There is something especially chilling and depressing about the girl's casual acceptance of mutual incomprehensibility when, weeks later, she explains how they "got real pissed and danced. In the driveway. Oh, my God. don't laugh" (9). It is impossible to justify all of the "shit" the "old guy" gave them: "There was more to it, and she was trying to get it talked out. After a time, she quit trying" (10). As in "Collectors" from *Will You Please Be Quiet, Please?* human nature abhors the vacuum that a lifetime of accumulated crap cannot dispel. But the assessment stops there. There is no satisfactory *telling*, so people quit trying to word their urgencies. Implosions hardly make a sound.

Implicit in the title of the next story, "Viewfinder," is not only the recurrence of the theme of voyeurism but, more generally, the adoption of a measured outlook: a viewfinder stabilizes and regulates by establishing a manageable range of perception. "A man without hands came to the door to sell me a photograph of my house" (11); with allegorical insistence the man's chrome hooks and the peculiar offer he brings combine to unsettle the narrator and deprive him of any feeling of at-homeness. Moreover, since the narrator confesses that he had himself been secretly inspecting his visitor through the window, they have actually been casing one another, each man a captive of the other's suspicions.

As in "Why Don't You Dance?" the radical readjustment of one's habitat awakens buried grudges and recriminations: "It made me think, seeing myself like that. I can tell you, it makes a man think" (12). The handicapped man brusquely dismisses the question of how he lost his hands and instead delivers empathy like a sales pitch. Like Robinson, the officious mailman in "What Do You Do in San Francisco?" he homes in on loneliness, intuiting a connection between the obscure family treacheries he himself has suffered and the narrator's predicament. To be sure, even as his host proposes that he take more pictures, the man targets the narrator's situation with sublime accuracy: " 'It won't work,' the man said. 'They're not coming back' " (14).

WHAT WE TALK ABOUT WHEN WE TALK ABOUT LOVE

What does a breach of etiquette matter between the abandoned?

Nevertheless his host does prevail upon him. He helps him into his prosthetic contraption (bringing to mind the strange commiseration of the gangly Bible salesman who marvels at Hulga's wooden leg in Flannery O'Connor's "Good Country People") and directs him to snap pictures of a variety of poses, culminating with his "shooting" the narrator as he perches on his roof. They wave to one another: hooks and hands in mirrored gestures of approval. But the exhilaration of having achieved this vantage on his domain is dampened when the narrator discovers that his roof is strewn with rocks that kids have heaved up there, apparently having tried to "score" through the chimney hole. Therefore, having found a view he prizes, he determines to purge it of contaminants: the story concludes with his hurling rocks off his roof and calling down for photographic evidence of his having taken charge. Despite the warning of the man without hands, a self-appointed patron saint of stunted contacts, that "motion shots" are not in his repertoire, the narrator continues in his campaign against the victimization he has endured and which the occasion of this new acquaintance has just revealed to him. With surprising, and probably unprecedented, fury he assails his own history.

"Mr. Coffee and Mr. Fixit" is related by a man who is comparatively matter-of-fact about his tribulations. "I've seen some things" (17), he confides, and in the space of about a thousand words he checks off an impressive series of betrayals and burdens. His speech is fragmented, hard-boiled, designed to keep his edge in the face of his mother's "putting out," his father's death, his wife's adultery, and everybody's drinking. Ironically, he sympathizes with his wife's lover, the so-called Mr. Fixit, who is, if possible, a more egregious loser than the fellow he wrongs. The narrator even admires Mr. Fixit's resourcefulness and appreciates their commonality: "I think maybe Myrna really loved the man. But he also had a little something on the side—a twenty-two-year-old named Beverly. Mr. Fixit did okay for a little guy who wore a button-up sweater" (19). Instead of feeling indignation—how belittling to be abused by so unprepossessing a person as Mr. Fixit!—he admires his pluck. Furthermore, when he talks about Mr. Fixit's having been laid off from his aerospace job (about which Mr. Fixit tells stories to enchant the narrator's daughter), he grows more compassionate toward his wife, going so far as to assume that her lover is bright in order to compliment her taste.

All of this was three years ago, he declares in an effort to prove his distance from all that "craziness": "I don't know what we were thinking of in those days" (18). But we see precious little evidence of future repair in his relationship with Myrna:

"Honey," I said to Myrna the night she came home. "Let's hug awhile and then you fix us a real nice supper."

Myrna said, "Wash your hands" (20).

Myrna is still critical, still stingy with her affections. Perhaps the reason that her husband had so readily pegged the feckless Mr. Fixit is that they shared not only the same woman but the same failures. His eagerness to forgive Myrna strikes her as a vulgar display of neediness that exasperates her. Certainly there will be no discussion of the matter.

In "Gazebo" once again the end of betrayal is silence. Duane and Holly had sought to establish a foothold by managing a motel, but Duane's adulterous routine with the maid demolishes that plan. In place of explanations Duane offers a litany of excuses about the incomprehensibility of everything that has befallen them: "I'd open my eyes and listen to [the phone] ring and wonder at what was happening to us" (22); "Then one morning, I don't know" (23); "Anyway, one thing and the other" (24); "This is awful. I don't know what is going to happen to me or to anyone else in the world" (24). Verbal and emotional incompetence undermines responsible behavior. Pent-up urges erupt into unpredictable, pointless mutinies: "That morning she pours Teacher's over my belly and licks it off. That afternoon she tries to jump out of the window" (21).

The moment Duane and Holly concede that they have irreparably "fouled" their lives (25), the tide of desolation overcomes them. They seal themselves up inside their motel, stop answering the phone or responding to the blare of car horns, and let it all go to seed, as if to corroborate their judgment upon themselves. There is something oddly invigorating at first about their surrender: "There was this funny thing of anything could happen now that we realized everything had" (27). Unfortunately, this is nothing to build on. Holly recalls an idyllic old farmhouse they had once passed—a place of easy good will and romantic ceremony where people maintained a natural dignity that weathered the hazards of the modern age. That had been her dream, to transplant that image to their motel. Thus "Gazebo" sounds the same self-pitying refrain that dominates the collection. While Duane feels "all out of words inside" (25), Holly needs only utter his name for him to take it as a sign that it—everything, now—is too late.

As in "The Idea" and "The Student's Wife" in *Will You Please Be Quiet, Please?* a wakeful night is the setting for "I Could See the Smallest Things." The similarities among these stories also include the fact that the insomniac must bear the insomnia alone. The narrator of "I Could See the Smallest Things" thinks that she has heard her gate move, but the electric, anticipatory atmosphere never rouses her comatose husband. She goes to the window to witness the spectral moon—"Any damn fool could imagine a face there"—and the metamorphic power of its stark light: "Everything lay in moonlight, and I could see the smallest things. The clothespins on the line, for instance" (31). While Cliff snores on, she accepts the "dare" and goes out to confront a world of x-ray visions. She is surprised by Sam Lawton, their neighbor and Cliff's one-time drinking companion, who is leaning over the fence; he too has been transfigured by the eerie moonlight. She feels unaccountably primed for adventure, simultaneously heady and exposed: "It felt funny walking around outside in my nightgown and my robe. I thought to myself that I should try to remember this, walking around outside like this" (33).

Sam initiates her into the slimy aspect of "the smallest things" by pointing out the pestilence of slugs at their feet; he has ventured out repeatedly to douse them with powdered poison. She is mesmerized by the procedure of detection and by the thriving underworld reality that pulses beneath her: "A plane passed overhead. I imagined the people on it sitting belted in their seats, some of them reading, some of them staring down at the ground" (34). Her conversation with Sam, seemingly their first interchange in years, suggests the tentative curiosity of aliens.

Returning to her bed, she looks at her pale, sluglike husband; perhaps she recognizes a metaphorical lesson in the story of how Sam's first wife had died of "heart failure." Struck with the thought of the smallest things outside, and the smallness of things within, she decides she has "to hurry up and sleep" (36), invoking oblivion like a benevolent spirit to chase away consciousness.

"The Bath" expands on one of those back-page dramas that leave people shaking their heads at the breakfast table. A woman meticulously directs a baker in the preparation of a cake for her son's eighth birthday. He is all business: "No pleasantries, just this small exchange, the barest information, nothing that was not necessary" (48). His abrupt matter-of-factness and her earnestness about this little celebration combine to create the false security of a prosaic situation.

Meanwhile, misfortune lurks with predatory dependability, as once again Carver compacts a supremely charged moment within a sober, inconspicuous literary style. On his way to school with his friend, Scotty is knocked down by a car. He gets up and departs for home, where he explains what happened to his mother, then lies down. Eventually the plans for the party dissolve and are replaced by an anxious vigil at the hospital. Driving home for a respite her husband wonders how he has gotten away with his relative contentment until now: "There had been work, fatherhood, family. The man had been lucky and happy. But fear made him want a bath" (49). Rectitude has proven a useless stay against tragedy. At home the father contends with the thudding irony of the baker's indignant phone call about a birthday cake that had not been picked up.

The balance of "The Bath" exhibits the frailty of the psychological defenses of the mother and father against Scotty's rapid decline. They cannot imagine how to recuperate familiar means of interaction, now disqualified:

The husband sat in the chair beside her. He wanted to say something else. But there was no saying what it should be. He took her hand and put it in his

lap. This made him feel better. It made him feel he
was saying something (52–3).

They have no words to contend with the immensity of
"shock," "scan," "coma"—the vocabulary of a fate they
dare not pronounce. When the distraught mother decides to go home to get cleaned up, she discovers that
any wrong turn in the hospital lands her in someone
else's harbored pain. In Carver's daily news tragedy is
unremarkable, devastation routine. Mrs. Weiss goes
home, feeds the dog, brews some tea, and waits for the
inevitable call that will confirm her dread.

The violence that emerges at the conclusion of "Tell
the Women We're Going" is just as inexplicable. Bill
and Jerry lead parallel lives, sharing the same clothes
and girls, the same disdain for their bosses, the same
modest dream of buying a better car. Their macho solidarity runs to callousness and profanity; however, at
twenty-two they are already feeling the clutches of age.
They sense that their accomplishments—marriage and
kids, Jerry's position as assistant manager at Robby's
Mart and Bill's at the plant—are really entrapments. "A
guy's got to get out" (60) is their creed of distraction,
which justifies anything from drinking and shooting
pool to cheating on their wives—all part of the manly
art of self-escape.

Part of that "art" entails treating women as objects
of desire and aggression (the two urges are insepar-
able). As the title of the story implies, even their wives
are categorized as species unspecific, just like the girls

on bicycles whom Jerry and Bill cruise past: " 'Look at that!' Jerry said, slowing, 'I could use some of that' " (61). If the girls were to repel their advances, they would be "bitches," and while the game is afoot, they are good "pieces"; obviously, neither designation elevates them.

The men manage to stop the girls and elicit their names and destination—sufficient victories to promise sexual successes to come. Despite Bill's uncertainty, Jerry persuades him to pursue the girls to Picture Rock, where they climb up the hill path to cut them off. Jerry's appetite and Bill's uneasiness mount with the effort:

> Bill had just wanted to fuck. Or even see them naked. On the other hand, it was okay with him if it didn't work out.
> He never knew what Jerry wanted. But it started and ended with a rock. Jerry used the same rock on both girls, first on the girl called Sharon and then on the one supposed to be Bill's (66).

Instantly the flimsy veneer of respectability they had erected for themselves disintegrates. Whether Jerry's act is premeditated or out of what half-sense of vengeance it originates, Bill "never knew," nor does he surmise his own motives for being there. There might be more of these vindictive outbursts in Carver's stories; certainly it is enervation, not satisfaction, that militates against them.

Fate's ambush is subtler but more prolonged in "After the Denim," in which an elderly couple, James and Edith Parker, play bingo at the community center as part of life's quiet endgame. Carver's characteristic reserve postpones the reader's appreciation of Edith's fatal ailment. Nevertheless, the laconic relationship depicted in "After the Denim" is not one of wordless disaffection—the awful norm in *What We Talk About When We Talk About Love*. On the contrary, it shows the natural, even sentimental, closeness of two people who have been together so long that they can anticipate one another without the promptings of extended conversation.

As it does in Ralph Ellison's "King of the Bingo Game," Bingo symbolizes the arbitrary rewards and indignities that fate can bestow.[6] The variations of the game—Blackout, Progressive—carry prophetic weight. To be sure, there is no justice evident in the world at any level: a cheater profits and a vulgar young couple, ignorant of the canons of play, win the biggest payoff of the evening. Meanwhile, the devoted James cannot hit any numbers at all, while Edith stoically bears her illness. With fortune so capricious, so set against him, James castigates the void:

Why not someone else? Why not those people tonight? Why not all those people who sail through life free as birds? Why not them instead of Edith? (77).

If only they had to sit with him in the waiting room! He'd tell them what to expect! He'd set those floozies straight! He'd tell them that what was waiting for you after the denim and the earrings, after touching each other and cheating at games (77).

The evanescent ease of "After the Denim" is succeeded by the beleaguerment of good people who ask for nothing more than a bit of unsullied happiness . . . but no such luck.

Carver resumes his examination of marital hand-to-hand combat in "A Serious Talk." The story takes place after the breakup of Burt and Vera. Although he returns to the house for Christmas with his family, Burt quickly realizes that, for them, the holiday has become an empty ceremony; there is nothing to celebrate.[7] Competing injuries—her habitual betrayals, his petty retaliations—make each utterance, even the most innocuous civility, an attack. Burt privately entertains extravagant illusions of restoration, but these seem feeble and juvenile next to their needs:

He considered her robe catching fire, him jumping up from the table, throwing her down onto the floor and rolling her over and over into the living room, where he would cover her with his body. Or should he run to the bedroom for a blanket? (108).

Increasing desperation moves him to ludicrous displays. For example, he dumps unidentifiable cigarette butts out of *their* ashtray (which he will swipe later on) and replaces them with his own. When Vera receives a personal phone call in the other room, Burt methodically cuts the phone cord with a carving knife. Of course, these clumsy attempts to reestablish his "claim" by severing her connections with the other man prove how beyond their means a serious talk would be. "There were things he wanted to say, grieving things, consoling things, things like that" (111). Instead, animosities close in to occupy the space vacated by meaningful speech:

> He left through the patio door. He was not certain, but he thought he had proved something. He hoped he had made something clear. The thing was, they had to have a serious talk soon. There were things that needed talking about, important things that had to be discussed. They'd talk again. Maybe after the holidays were over and things got back to normal. He'd tell her the goddamn ashtray was a goddamn dish, for example (112–13).

Relations are always tenuous at best in a cold war.

"The Calm" earns an instant's relief from the oppressive climate of *What We Talk About When We Talk About Love*. The narrator is getting a haircut when one of the waiting customers, whom he recognizes as the local bank guard, launches into a tale of his deer-hunting adventure with his father and his son. It is neither a lesson of comradeship among the generations nor a tribute to nature's splendor. Hung over and nauseous, the boy had fired wildly in the direction of an old buck that had emerged from the underbrush; his father, the bank guard, managed to "stun" him with a gut shot, but the buck escaped. When it grew too hot to trail him, they assumed the coyotes or the buzzards had finished him off. Obscenity and anger pervade the bank guard's story; hunting brought out no majesty in him, only the same atavistic release as fighting in Korea. Enraged by his failure, he cursed and cuffed his son. Then, when it turned out that the grandfather had killed the buck on his own, he responded by ridiculing the "little bastard." By now he is so worked up that a snide comment by an older customer in the shop leads the bank guard to threaten to take him on. Finally, the barber brings order to the situation. A traditional bastion of serenity, the small-town barber shop is presumed to be sacred and no place for unfriendliness. Through his cunning art— the narrator compares his tenderness to a lover's—the barber fashions a still point in the turning world, to which the narrator has the privilege of access even now:

But today I was thinking of that place, of Crescent City, and of how I was trying out a new life there with my wife, and how, in the barber's chair that morning, I had made up my mind to go. I was thinking today about the calm I felt when I closed my eyes and let the barber's fingers move through my hair, the sweetness of those fingers, the hair already starting to grow (121).

WHAT WE TALK ABOUT WHEN WE TALK ABOUT LOVE

The volume's title story extends the theme of the heart's perpetual commotion by updating and burlesquing Plato's *Symposium*. "What We Talk About When We Talk About Love" also features the most expansive conversationalists in this collection: Mel and Terri, both of whom are married for the second time and both sporting scars from their first marriages, and Nick (the narrator) and Laura, newlyweds who are still in the throes of a mutual romantic trance. Mel and Terri carry on the bulk of the gin-induced discussion of love, whereas Nick and Laura are more equivocal and seem content to placate their friends or to reassure one another with intimate gestures.

Mel and Terri propose divergent definitions of "real love." A cardiologist who once spent five years studying in a seminary, Mel contends that love is a spiritual phenomenon whose pinnacle was and continues to be the chivalric code. Terri, on the other hand, argues that the brutality of her first husband, Ed, displayed the formidableness of his passion for her. As the conversation gains momentum, contradictions surface in their testimonies. Mel, the self-proclaimed spiritual scientist, confesses his daydreams about murdering his first wife that parallel Terri's grotesque tales of her relationship with Ed. Meanwhile, Terri grows increasingly anxious about redeeming her volatile past, even at the expense of offending her present husband: " 'He did love me though, Mel. Grant me that,' Terri said. 'That's all I'm asking. He didn't love me the way you love me. I'm not saying that. But he loved me. You can grant me that, can't you?' " (140).

The greatest obstacle to any ideal of love turns out to be the transitoriness of love. After all, both Mel and Terri had vowed allegiance to their original partners, so what is there to prevent the same deterioration from happening again? Ironically, the "saving grace" of love (145) is its elasticity—one can move one from divorce or tragedy and love anew—but this is further evidence against love's absolute status and hollows out current protestations of devotion. In other words, love's transient nature could be either its vindication or its vanquishment—the source of its preciousness or its untrustworthiness. Consequently, the very situation that the four friends occupy as they conduct their leisurely talking and drinking around the dinner table is shown to have the same fragile charms as the subject at hand:

The afternoon sun was like a presence in this room, the spacious light of ease and generosity. We could have been anywhere, somewhere enchanted. We raised our glasses again and grinned at each other like children who had agreed on something forbidden (144).

The relative articulateness of these characters by no means enables them to reach a satisfactory conclusion, and as a result Mel suggests that "it ought to make us feel ashamed when we talk like we know what we're talking about when we talk about love" (146). In this way, Mel echoes Pausanias' declaration in *The Sympo-sium*: "I do not think, Phaidros, that the rules were properly laid down, I mean that we should just simply belaud Love. For if Love were one, that would do, but really he is not one; and since he is not one, it is more proper to say first which we are to praise."[8]

Mel's crowning point regarding the spiritual core of love recalls Holly's envious vision of the dignified inti-macy of the old people she encountered in "Gazebo." Mel relates how, after a terrible automobile accident, an old man and woman lay barely alive in their hospital beds; they were completely covered by casts and ban-dages. However, despite his horrible injuries, the hus-band was primarily depressed because he could not see his wife through the tiny eyeholes in his bandages. By this time Mel has grown rather drunk and profane, and his testiness toward Terri belies his argument. So, too, is his chivalric hero, the medieval knight, tarnished by the admission that he often suffocated in his armor; moreover, his protective gear was also a measure of his inaccessibility. Finally, when Mel fantasizes about arriv-ing in the guise of a beekeeper (helmeted, anonymous, and padded from head to toe) at the house of his first wife in order to release a swarm of bees, he modernizes and disqualifies the knight's noble image.

Nick and Laura come close to embodying a simple yet profound enjoyment of one another's company, but when Nick ostentatiously kisses Laura's hand, Mel and Terri find it more amusing than tender. They all toast to "true love," but Terri's gentle admonishment to Laura—

"Wait awhile" (143)—suggests that time misses no one in its assault on affection. Rating the quality of the consolation that remains at the end of the story depends upon to what extent the elusive, unpredictable, hazardous process of love compensates for the skewering of the romantic ideal (upon which the discussants cannot agree anyway). In the darkened room, silent save for "the human noise we sat there making" (154), perhaps these moments together, deeply imbued with shared sensibilities, make up for the antagonisms, the regrets, the flirtations, the spilled gin.

"One More Thing," the volume's postscript story, reprises the fundamental plight of distance in concentrated form. There is the unemployed, belligerent husband, who ignites at the slightest provocation; there is the overworked, reproachful wife, who shows the wear and tear of having had to put up and bear up for so long. L. D. drinks too much and channels his exasperations at his daughter, Rae, who has refused to attend school for weeks: "Maxine said it was another tragedy in a long line of low-rent tragedies" (156).

In his foreword to William Kittredge's *We Are Not in This Together*, Carver writes about the absence of poetry in the lives of characters whose obligations outweigh their interpersonal resources:

Maybe there was a little, once, in the beginning, but then something happened—it was worked out of you, or beaten out of you, or you drank too much, too long, and it left you; and now you're worse off than ever because you still have to go through the motions, even though you know it's for nothing now, a senseless reminder of better days.[9]

What results is an overwhelming sense of urgency without object that leads to spurious acts of defiance. In "One More Thing," Rae explains how every illness is really in the mind and L. D. calls her crazy; Maxine walks in on their argument and bemoans the craziness that she must come home to. L. D. hurls a jar of pickles through the kitchen window, and the women huddle to protect one another from the crazy man in their midst. When L. D. roughly packs to move out, he blames everything on having had to live in "this nuthouse" (159). There is always one more thing—one more complaint or tribulation or unspeakable need—and Carver's murderously spare prose reaches these people just in time to pronounce their defeat:

> L. D. put the shaving bag under his arm and picked up the suitcase.
> He said, "I just want to say one more thing."
> But then he could not think what it could possibly be (159).

In *What We Talk About When We Talk About Love,* ferocities fade to a whimper of discontent.

Notes

1. Adam Mars-Jones, "Words for the Walking Wounded," *Times Literary Supplement* 22 Jan. 1982: 76.

2. Mona Simpson, interview, "The Art of Fiction LXXVI," *Paris Review* 25 (1983)): 210. Carver goes on to complain about the validity of the term *minimalist* to designate this aesthetic.

3. Reprinted from *Furious Seasons* are "Sacks" (originally "The Fling"), "The Third Thing That Killed My Father Off" ("Dummy"), "Everything Stuck to Him" ("Distance"), "Popular Mechanics" ("Mine"), and "So Much Water So Close to Home."

4. Carver tells the genesis of "Why Don't You Dance" in the *Paris Review* interview: "I was visiting some writer friends in Missoula back in the mid-1970s. We were all sitting around drinking and someone told a story about a barmaid named Linda who got drunk with her boyfriend one night and decided to move all of her bedroom furnishings into the backyard. . . . And after the guy finished telling the story, someone said, "Well, who's going to write it?" I don't know who else might have written it, but I wrote it. Not then, but later. About four or five years later, I think. . . . Actually, it was the first story I wrote after I finally stopped drinking" (208).

5. *What We Talk About When We Talk About Love* (New York: Knopf, 1981) 4. Subsequent references to stories in this volume are noted parenthetically in the text.

6. Ralph Ellison, "King of the Bingo Game," *The Norton Anthology of Short Fiction*, ed. R. V. Cassill, 3rd ed. (New York: Norton, 1986) 423–31.

7. In the *Paris Review* interview Carver notes how "A Serious Talk" was initiated by a line he had heard while drunk: "That's the last Christmas you'll ever ruin for us!" He later combined this line with "other things I imagined, imagined so accurately that they *could* have happened" (206).

8. "The Symposium," *Great Dialogues of Plato*, ed. Eric H. Warmington and Philip G. Rouse, trans. W. H. D. Rouse (New York: New American Library, 1956) 78. Diotima's analysis of Love for Socra-

tes' benefit similarly portends the contrary attitudes of Mel and Terri when Diotima explains that Love, as the son of Plenty and Poverty, is inherently problematical (99).

9. Raymond Carver, foreword, *We Are Not in This Together*, by William Kittredge. (Port Townsend, WA: Graywolf, 1984) ix.

CHAPTER FIVE

Cathedral

"I knew I'd gone as far the other way as I could or wanted to go, cutting everything down to the marrow, not just to the bone."[1] In this way Carver announces a deliberate departure from the relentless austerity of *What We Talk About When We Talk About Love* in favor of the "fleshed out" fictions of *Cathedral*. "Generous" is the term of approval employed by several reviewers to recognize the ventilation of the claustrophobic method and attitude that heretofore had dominated Carver's work. Perhaps befitting the increased stability and ease in Carver's personal life, the strapped constituents of Carver country breathe a bit more freely in this volume.[2]

Nevertheless, the majority of the stories dispute any claim to a fundamental break from the tenor of the three preceding collections. While there is impressive evidence in *Cathedral* of his having begun to transcend the haplessness and brittle restraint that commonly besets his characters, Carver by no means forsakes the "down to the marrow" aesthetic that governed his earlier col-

CATHEDRAL

lections. It may prove instructive, then, to contrast those stories in *Cathedral* that adhere to the established style with those that signal an opening out into what could be termed a postminimalist direction.

"Feathers" teases the reader with the prospect of meaningful repair in the lives of Jack and Fran only to capitulate to the pervading despair of previous volumes. Jack's first-person narrative turns out to be a prolonged complaint about the irredeemable leakage of time, which is temporarily disguised by the comic conditions of a dinner party at Bud and Olla's. The invitation by his friend at work had originally seemed to Jack to be little more than an opportunity to break the boredom, but in retrospect it stands forth in his mind as the final incident commemorating the halcyon days of his marriage:

That evening at Bud and Olla's was special. I knew it was special. That evening I felt good about almost everything in my life. I couldn't wait to be alone with Fran to talk to her about what I was feeling. I made a wish that evening. Sitting there at the table, I closed my eyes for a minute and thought hard. What I wished for was that I'd never forget or otherwise let go of that evening. That's one wish of mine that came true. And it was bad luck that for me that it did. But, of course, I couldn't know that then.[3]

Jack recalls, or revises, that early period of his marriage as a time when innocence was a kind of enclave for him and Fran; they felt complete unto themselves and believed they needed neither children nor outside acquaintances to complicate their love. Looking back over the narrative, however, as the fast-forward conclusion of "Feathers" requires the reader to do, exposes intimations of the impending estrangement of Jack and Fran.[4] Their insistence upon self-sufficiency, for example, appears to be a shield against incursions that would expose the fragility of their relationship, while their routine discussions of things they wish for but never expect to have—a new car, a vacation in Canada, a place in the country—come to suggest more profound deficiencies.

Having declared her reluctance to accept the dinner invitation, Fran is openly contemptuous of Bud and Olla's lower-class home in "the sticks." To be sure, Bud and Olla are unrefined to say the least: their furnishings are vulgar, their conversation coarse, and their life style utterly unfettered by pretension or taste. Still, they are friendly and as hospitable as their means and manners allow; moreover, the unselfconscious happiness they share makes them invulnerable to disdain.

Jack and Fran, on the other hand, are helpless in the face of confusion or crisis. When upon their arrival Bud and Olla's pet peacock, a huge, ungainly bird, lands in front of their car, their mutual ineptitude shows through:

"My God," Fran said quietly. She moved her hand over to my knee.

"Goddamn," I said. There was nothing else to say (8).

Awe, anger, and bewilderment constitute the full store of their reactions.

The evening is marked by the contrast between the pinched behavior of Jack and Fran, and the natural, if uncultivated, good will of their hosts. While Jack worries that he is overdressed for the occasion, Fran barely manages to hide her contempt, which is revealed most markedly as she watches a televised stock car race with the men: "maybe one of those damn cars will explode right in front of us," Fran said. "Or else maybe one'll run up into the grandstand and smash the guy selling crummy hot dog's" (11). At first Jack attributes her attitude to the fact that "the day was shot" in the weird company of Bud and Olla, but upon reflection at the end of "Feathers," it appears to have been a sign of a more comprehensive impatience that Jack failed to interpret fully.

However, nothing fazes Bud and Olla; even potentially uncomfortable subjects they themselves introduce (about their money problems or her father's death) are smoothly incorporated into the fabric of their abiding love for one another. The plaster cast of Olla's twisted teeth commemorating the eventual miracle of orthodontia, and which sits on top of the television set like a prized relic, is a source of shared enthusiasm over their progress: "That's one of the things I'm thankful for. I keep them around to remind me how much I owe Bud"

(13). The stalking peacock, which has free reign over their roof and yard and which is welcome inside the house to play with the baby, may strike their guests as forbidding, but "Joey" is one more member of the family. If Joey does not possess the transfiguring divinity of Flannery O'Connor's bird of paradise in "The Displaced Person," his scaled-down majesty earns no less devotion from Bud and Olla; meanwhile, for Fran and Jack the aggressive peacock symbolizes their harassment.

In short, Bud and Olla do not depend on the meager gestures of charity that their guests can muster. Even the astonishing ugliness of their squalling baby—"Even calling it ugly does it credit," Jack confides (20)—cannot affect Bud and Olla's domestic pride. Indeed, the child makes Fran feel deprived; she grows wistful about seeing her niece in Denver. Holding and playing with him triggers her plea to Jack later that night, which is reminiscent of Mary's urgent desire to be "diverted" at the close of "What's in Alaska?": "Honey, fill me up with your seed!" (25).

But the child they ultimately produce does not avail them, and the marriage tenses, then unravels. Fran quits her job, puts on weight, cuts her luxurious hair that Jack had adored. She habitually curses the episode at Bud and Olla's as though they had caused the downfall of Fran and Jack's last stand of innocence. Jack becomes sullen and uncommunicative—"We don't talk about it. What's to say?" (26)—and increases his distance from Bud at the plant. Whereas Bud brags about his son, Jack merely says that everyone at home is fine and broods about the fact that his boy "has a conniving streak in him" (26). The unexpected detour that "Feathers" takes preempts the story's apparent development toward the verge of reconstituted love; as a result, every detail of the dinner party becomes an ironic portent of present desolation.

Seduction by hope intensifies marital vulnerability. In "Chef's House," as in "Feathers," futility surfaces like some awful genetic code. Wes convinces his estranged wife to relinquish the life she has been building apart from him in favor of rejoining him as he struggles to recover from alcoholism. Currently living in a rented house with an ocean view, Wes tells Edna that he needs her to complete his self-reclamation project. Although their children keep their distance, Wes and Edna spend a good summer together, and Edna, who narrates the story, confides that she has begun to believe in their solidarity again. The inevitable crisis comes in the form of Chef, who returns to ask them to vacate the premises. (He wants the house back for his daughter, who has lost her husband.) Immediately they sense that whatever they have been restoring is counterfeit, that defeat has rooted them out of hiding.

Baffled by the injustice of it all, Wes also feels oddly confirmed in his original definition of his limited expectations, and he suddenly finds himself beyond the reach of his wife's consoling:

Then I said something. I said, Suppose, just suppose, nothing had ever happened. Suppose this

was for the first time. Just suppose. It doesn't hurt to
suppose. Say none of the other had ever happened.
You know what I mean? Then what? I said.

Wes fixed his eyes on me. He said, Then I suppose
we'd have to be somebody else if that was the case.
Somebody we're not. I don't have that kind of
supposing left in me. We were born who we are. Don't
you see what I'm saying? (31–32).

It *does* hurt to suppose, for supposing deludes Carver's
characters into fantasies that burst at the slightest insti-
gation; such is the pathology of surrender. Edna cannot
hold out for long against her husband's logic, and she
ends up absorbing his attitude. The same sort of "I
should have known better" tonal quality rules both
"Feathers" and "Chef's House"; in both cases reform is
too demanding to imagine into existence. For Carver to
bother to extend "Chef's House" to include verification
of Wes's relapse and Edna's final renunciation would be
redundant.

Uncontrollable circumstances claim two more victims in "Preservation." Three months of unemployment
has steeped Sandy's husband in the same funk as Wes.
He has essentially given up the fight, so he spends his
days lazing on the sofa, an emblem of his surrender:
"That goddamn sofa! As far as she was concerned, she
didn't even want to sit on it again. She couldn't imagine them ever having lain down there in the past to
make love" (37). His unstated justification may be that
because man cannot prevail, he must learn how to en-

dure; therefore, he adopts a posture of equanimity that Sandy finds maddening. When she happens upon his book *Mysteries of the Past*, and reads about a man discovered in a peat bog after two thousand years, her husband's petrified figure comes readily to mind.

When their freezer gives out, they are surrounded with perishables on all sides—a precise image of their own domestic entropy. Sandy frantically prepares to cook up as much as possible before everything spoils, but her husband is not up to any exertion and drops off to sleep on the sofa. She considers the prospects for finding a decent used freezer at an auction, but she can only sustain enthusiasm on her own for so long. The sight of her barefoot husband standing in the water puddling from the useless freezer once again recalls the preserved corpse from *Mysteries of the Past*: "She knew she'd never in her life see anything so unusual. But she didn't know what to make of it yet" (46). In predictable Carver fashion, Sandy's inarticulateness completes her bondage.[5]

The expense of psychological and verbal repression is evidenced in the airless interior monologue of "The Compartment," whose title metaphor connotes the main character's predicament of self-containment without self-sufficiency. Myers is traveling by train to visit his son at the university in Strasbourg. It has been eight years since their last contact. A letter from his son, whose signature included "love," has initiated the flicker of optimism that has enabled Myers to subdue, for the moment, his suspicion that the boy had been guilty of "malign interference" between his parents, thereby hastening their violent separation.

Myers's unease about the impending meeting fills him with ambivalence, for the clutch of past irritations and blame continues to oppress him. Furthermore, in the intervening eight years Myers has not changed for the better. His aloofness, which is intimated to be one of the principal reasons behind his failed relationships, has intensified, as suggested by the fact that in planning his vacation he could barely imagine anyone whom he might have informed of his absence. His insularity is also documented by the meagerness of his leisure—he reads books on waterfowl decoys—as well as by his aspiration to live "in an old house surrounded by a wall" (48). He envies the man who shares his railcar because his inability to speak English and his talent for sleep combine to ensure his inviolability. Meanwhile, Myers passes the time by perusing guidebooks about places he has already visited and regretting that he had not gotten to reading them before—a situation that precisely parallels his belatedness in familial affairs.

Briefly put, Myers is a man trapped in the conditional tense. His European vacation has been contaminated from the beginning by his self-imposed segregation. He feels isolated and maladaptive in the most exotic cities, and about as spontaneous as a spider. The prospect of encountering his son at the train station sets off a prolonged series of calculations, as though he were a foreign ambassador uncertain of the local amenities: "Maybe the boy would say a few words—*I'm glad to*

see you—how was your trip? And Myers would say—
something. He really didn't know what he was going to
say" (50).

Because he cannot envision the future, Myers is
mired in his troubled past. The climax of "The Compartment" comes when he discovers that the gift he had
bought for his son, the watch he was keeping in his coat
pocket, has been stolen. He ludicrously tries to intuit
who the thief is, but this only increases his humiliation
and anger. He is helpless among foreigners; the inva-
sion of his privacy confirms for him that the entire adventure has been a mistake. He realizes that he had not
wanted to see his son, that somehow their true enmity
had been obscured.

Myers does not get off the train at the Strasbourg
station. He watches a romantic parting at the platform,
but is careful to avoid being seen by his son, who is
probably waiting there for him. Nor does he have the
courage to ask the conductor if the train's next destination is Paris. Indeed, Myers is a man for whom *any* contact seems like "malign interference." Lost in regret, he
wanders onto the wrong railcar while his own is un-
coupled. Even Myers himself recognizes this last em-
barrassment as representative of the dissociation that
defines him. His belongings gone, surrounded by strangers whose appearance, language, and joviality exclude
him, Myers wanders down the maze of tracks: "For a
moment, Myers had the impression of the landscape
shooting away from him. He was going somewhere, he
knew that. And if it was the wrong direction, sooner or

later he'd find it out" (58). Sleep finally arrives like a benediction.

The husband in "Vitamins" is just as exasperating as Sandy's. In response to his wife's ranting about how she detests her job coordinating a group of young women who sell vitamins door to door—even her dreams are infected by vitamins, she bitterly complains—he recoils into muteness. He has a "nothing job" of his own as a hospital janitor; however, instead of commiserating with Patti about her misery, he rationalizes making passes at her employees during a drunken party and, later, compelling one of them, Donna, to meet him on the sly.

This is familiar territory—trying to lose one's guilt in tawdriness, to court oblivion like a lover. He takes Donna to a "spade bar" he has frequented in the past, and once settled, they begin to grope one another with impunity. But their tryst is interrupted by the arrival of two black men who insinuate themselves at their booth. One of the men, Nelson, who has just returned home from Viet Nam, brags about the tactics of psychological warfare he had learned there and begins to practice them. He offers to display the prized shriveled ear he had cut from a corpse and startles them with sudden threats of violence. Most disturbing are his lewd offers to Donna to pay for her company, which he fortifies with suggestions that the man's wife is probably involved in some obscene relationship of her own even as they speak. In this way Nelson serves as a kind of vile conscience for the would-be lovers. They feel exposed, out of their depth; even though they manage to extricate themselves from the bar, Nelson's last remarks follow them: "He yelled, 'It ain't going to do no good! Whatever you do, it ain't going to help none!' " (107).

Sentenced to failure by this vulgar prophet, the unnamed husband and Donna recoil from one another into their respective justifications. He asks perfunctorily about her plans, but "right then she could have died of a heart attack and it wouldn't have meant anything" (108). She makes a clumsy effort at building a faith in a new beginning in Portland: "There must be something in Portland. Portland's on everybody's mind these days. Portland's a drawing card. Portland this, Portland that. Portland's as good a place as any. It's all the same" (108).

It is all the same for him as well when he comes home to Patti's rantings over yet another bad dream. Once again Carver demonstrates how attempts to escape confining routines merely reveal their viciousness and resiliency:

I couldn't take any more tonight. "Go back to sleep, honey. I'm looking for something." I said. I knocked some stuff out of the medicine chest. Things rolled into the sink. "Where's the aspirin?" I said. I knocked down some more things. I didn't care. Things kept falling (109).

He is assailed by gravity. From aimless anger, to furtive-ness, to apathy and resignation—so runs the course of private ruin.

In "Careful," Lloyd's cramped accommodations in Mrs. Matthews's boardinghouse are similar to Mr. Slater's "vacuumed" dwelling in "Collectors." Lloyd has neither clock nor telephone to trouble his womb-like limbo; out of work and alcoholic—his attempt to wean himself from hard liquor with cheap champagne now has him downing it by the bottle—he has diminished to a blur. In fact, he has grown so incurious about affairs outside his attic apartment that when one afternoon he passes his landlady's door and notices her collapsed on the floor, he "chooses" to assume she is asleep instead of injured or dead and hustles back to his quarters. Nor can he muster the energy to reflect about his "mildly crazy" habits for very long. "Then, the more he thought about it, the more he could see didn't matter much one way or the other. He'd had doughnuts and champagne for breakfast. So what?" (112–13).

On the day his wife, Inez, shows up for a serious discussion about their future, Lloyd is suffering from a blocked right ear. Their separation, a result of what Inez had termed an "assessment," has apparently been a tonic for her, for she arrives with new clothes and new vitality; she is set to thrive. For his part Lloyd is at the low point of his postpartum depression. As in "Chef's House," a wife's departure signals the imminence of collapse. With symbolic aptness his ear condition has upset his equilibrium and made it difficult to hear his wife. His head feels like a barrel in which his own solipsistic, self-pitying voice endlessly reverberates, which is a far cry from that time "long ago, when they used to feel they had ESP when it came to what the other was thinking. They could finish sentences that the other had started" (117). Now her cares and consolations spatter uselessly against him.

After failing with assorted and potentially hazardous implements to dislodge the buildup of wax, Inez seeks out Mrs. Matthews for help. She returns with baby oil, which she warms to pour into Lloyd's ear. Clearly her apprehensive husband is in need of supervision, and Inez's attentions are of necessity more maternal than wifely. ("Careful" sounds like the plea of a nervous child or a parent's gentle patronage.) Lying on his side to let the oil do its work, Lloyd feels helpless; his whole apartment seems out of whack.

Lloyd's ear finally opens, first to his delight, then to his dismay as he realizes that there is little he can do to stave off another such episode. Meanwhile, Inez consults with Mrs. Matthews in the hall; perhaps she is finalizing the transfer of the nursemaid role to the landlady. Due to the time lost to the crisis, she does not have the time to go into the subject that brought her here in the first place. In the end Inez escapes to other commitments, leaving Lloyd to contend with his inertia. But with his impacted condition—plugged up and mired in irresponsibility—Lloyd is not going anywhere at all.

"The Train" is Carver's sequel to John Cheever's story "The Five-Forty-Eight" (1958).[6] Cheever's story concerns the revenge of a secretary against her rather vile boss, Blake, who used her sexually only to fire her in order to escape further complications. She has exhibited signs of mental instability, and she now tracks her culprit to the train, where she accosts him, showing him that she is carrying a gun in her purse. Blake cannot elicit aid from the other passengers; with nightmarish poetic justice it turns out that the only other passengers around him are also people he has mistreated in the past. When he and his secretary are finally alone at the station, she makes him submit to a symbolic act of repentance and self-excoriation: he must drop to his knees and smother his face in the dirt. Nevertheless, his recriminations extend only so far as his fear of death; the woman's departure leaves no lesson or epiphany in its wake. Although he does seem to be more intensely aware of the tenuousness of what had always been the secure surroundings of Shady Hill, "he got to his feet and picked up his hat from the ground where it had fallen and walked home."[7]

Carver picks up the forgotten thread of Miss Dent, who is preparing for her trip back into the city. The model story is reimagined according to the spartan specifications of the Carver style: Miss Dent's complexities are contracted to a motiveless menace, and the thoughts of the woman who still carries the gun with which she has recently threatened a man are suspended by a matter-of-fact style that also inhibits the "gift for dreams" she had been credited as having in Cheever's rendition. Moreover, her plot is displayed by the indecipherable conversation of an old man and middle-aged woman who are sitting near Miss Dent in the station waiting room. Their absurd agitations invoke Miss Dent's sense of irony, and she considers what their reaction would be were she to inform them that she has a gun in her bag.

All of a sudden the couple converges on her with bizarre accusations:

"You don't say much," the woman said to Miss Dent. "But I'll wager you could say a lot if someone got you started. Couldn't you? But you're a sly boots. You'd rather just sit with your prim little mouth while other people talk their heads off. Am I right? Still waters. Is that your name?" (153).

Apparently Miss Dent is hardly manifested by her outrageous episode; every Carver character, after all, is the hero of some tragedy so supremely important that he cannot lend himself to another's.

As the anonymous passengers watch these three people board the train, "they felt sure that whatever these people's business had been that night, it had not come to a happy conclusion. But the passengers had seen things more various than this in their lifetime" (155). Everyone is a closet mystery, but the rampant preoccupation and self-interment of Carver's characters prohibit them from experiencing any more substantial intersection than this. It appears that Cheever's Blake,

who only enters "The Train" by implication, is unremarkable in his immunity to reflection. Furthermore,
since they are obsessed by their own stories, they "are
only lethargically aware that the world is diverse and
'filled with business of every sort,' " and they "cling to
the prejudice that they do not care to know more. They
can't be shouted at."[8] Its plot potential squandered,
"The Train" speeds off into the darkness.

The interest the narrator takes in the newly arrived
Minnesota family in "The Bridle" results from her suspicion that their bankruptcy mirrors her own sense of a
foreclosed future. Holits, his wife, Betty, and their two
sons have come to Arizona in search of better luck. As
comanager (with her husband, Harley) of the apartment
building, the narrator is concerned at first about
whether or not the new tenants will be responsible
about paying their rent, but she feels for their predicament; bad luck can come to anyone, and "no disgrace
can be attached to that" (191). Holits pays his rent and
damage deposit with fifty-dollar bills, and she is moved
to wonder about the "exotic" fates of the bills themselves as they pass from place to place and hand to
hand. Indeed, even her unfortunate tenants have the
advantage of *movement*; meanwhile, she is rooted to a
claustrophobic role, her life assigned to a gruff husband
who spends the day addicted to television and who
sleeps at night "like a grindstone" beside her (201).

Both as building manager and as a stylist (she abjures the term "beautician" as too old-fashioned), the
narrator presides over the sad little dramas that are

played out on the premises. These range from the pedestrian—bouts with alcohol, disaffection, and loneliness—to the wickedly cynical, as seen in the building party that features a drawing for an attorney's free divorce services. When Betty gets a split-shift waitressing job, she comes to the narrator for a dye job on her roots, and under the soothing influence of the hair stylist's care (paralleling the consequences of the barber's "sweet" art in "The Calm"), Betty confesses the history of her tribulations. She is Holits's second wife—his first wife ran out on him and the children. Holits bought a racehorse, which he named for Betty, and which he believed would be the instrument of their salvation. However, Fast Betty has proven to be a perennial loser, and mounting gambling losses as well as the cost of upkeep itself has sundered their dreams of "working toward something" (199). The narrator compliments Betty's cuticles, but it is meager solace for someone who is convinced that she is a long shot who will never finish in the money; she does not even bother to dream anymore. Cosmetic improvements—the dye job on her hair, the new job, the new residence—cannot change her essential entrapment.

After this episode Betty keeps away from the narrator for some time, and Holits also appears to have found employment, for he is seldom seen. The climax of the story occurs when during a drunken party with some of the other renters at poolside after closing hours, Holits tries to dive into the water from atop the cabana. He hits the deck, gashing his forehead. The narrator, incensed by the display (and probably by her exclusion from the group as well) rushes to the scene. The scene concludes with a blundering rush to the hospital, with Holits deliriously repeating his complaint: "I can't go it" (204). Significantly, Harley sleeps through the entire crisis.

"I can't go it": the phrase is an apt motto for Holits, for whom the crash to the deck is but one more in a line of downfalls. Betty quits her job to nurse him and Holits grows sullen and standoffish. Soon they are seen packing up for another move. Forever at a loss, they must believe in luck because, presumably, luck can change. Meanwhile, Harley has no compassion to waste on that "crazy Swede" and his family, and he settles back in front of the television as though "nothing has happened or ever will happen" (207). In a surprisingly rebellious exhibition, his wife inserts herself between Harley and his television screen, but she finds she has nothing whatsoever to say to him.

When she goes up to clean the vacated apartment, the narrator discovers Holits's bridle. Perhaps he forgot it. Perhaps he left it behind as part of a ceremony of divestiture in hopes of preparing the way for a different life. For the narrator the bridle is a clear symbol of restraint, of being controlled from without: "The bit's heavy and cold. If you had to wear this thing between your teeth, I guess you'd catch on in a hurry" (208). She knows what it is to be cruelly reined in, to be perpetually at the mercy of someone, or something, beyond the reach of reason.

CATHEDRAL

The stories discussed above follow the general tone established in Carver's three previous collections. The absence of recourse and the unnourished hopes shrunken to a grudge; the misfired social synapses and the implied ellipses like breadcrumb trails leading from breakdown to breakdown; the "preseismic" endings that "are inflected rather than inflicted upon us";[9] the speechless gaps where intimacies are supposed to go—these characteristics persist. On the other hand, some of the stories in *Cathedral* do suggest an opening out that indicates, however subtly, an ongoing evolution in Carver's art.

The reformulation of "The Bath" in *What We Talk About When We Talk About Love*) as "A Small, Good Thing" in *Cathedral* is an obvious place to begin to examine this contrast. Carver himself has indicated that the enhancement of the original story's "unfinished business" is so fundamental that they now seem to him to be two entirely different stories.[10] Certainly the structure of his sentences has been changed in several instances to be less fragmentary, less constrained. For example, while she is waiting for the arrival of the doctor in "The Bath," the mother's dread is nearly wordless, and absolutely privatized: "She was talking to herself like this. We're into something now, something hard."[11] In "A Small, Good Thing," however, Ann (she has been granted a name and a fuller identity, as have the other characters in the story) is presented as having a more extensively characterized consciousness, which is thus more sympathetic and accessible:

She stood at the window with her hands gripping the sill, and knew in her heart that they were into something now, something hard. She was afraid, and her teeth began to chatter until she tightened her jaws. She saw a big car stop in front of the hospital and someone, a woman in a long coat, get into the car. She wished she were that woman and somebody, anybody, was driving her away from here to somewhere else, a place where she would find Scotty waiting for her when she stepped out of the car, ready to say *Mom* and let her gather him in her arms.

In a little while, Howard woke up. He looked at the boy again. Then he got up from the chair, stretched, and went over to stand beside her at the window. They both stared at the parking lot. They didn't say anything. *But they seemed to feel each other's insides now, as though the worry had made them transparent in a perfectly natural way* (70–71; my italics).

With the expansion of the original version comes a development of the spiritual cost of the crisis. The result of every extension of detail in "A Small, Good Thing"— from the increased dimension of the baker when he is first introduced, to the transcendence of merely symbolic function of the black family at the hospital—is to decrease the distances that separate Carver's characters from one another and Carver's narrator from the story he relates. For one critic the expansion represents a movement away from "existential realism" toward a comparatively coherent, more dramatic, and more personal "humanistic realism."[12]

CATHEDRAL

Carver's most profound revision is to carry the plot beyond the state of abeyance of Scotty's coma. ("The Bath" concludes in the middle of the phone call, just before the "death sentence" is actually pronounced.) In "A Small, Good Thing," Scotty's death spasm occurs even as the doctor is discussing with the parents the surgery that he will perform to save the boy. Having been assured only the previous day that Scotty would recover, Ann and Howard are absolutely overwhelmed, and they dazedly prepare to withstand the autopsy, to call relatives. Under these more developed circumstances the baker's call is no longer just the ironic plot gimmickry it had been in "The Bath"; instead, his interruption of and ultimate participation in the family's loss in "A Small, Good Thing" precipitates the cycle of "dramatic recognition, reversal, confrontation, and catharsis" that finally gives the story the finished contours of tragedy—the "low-rent" tragic pattern fleshed out to classic dimensions.[13] Replacing the blank, dazed reaction of the anxious mother in the former version is her wild anger at the "evil bastard" who has blundered into their grief; when translated to the context of their open wound, his message about the birthday cake sounds ominous and malicious: " 'Your Scotty, I got him ready for you,' the man's voice said. 'Did you forget him?' " (83).

He hangs up, and only after a second call and hang-up does Ann realize that it must have been the baker. Blazing with outrage, desperate to strike out against their defeat, Ann and Howard drive to the shopping center bakery for a showdown. The baker, menacingly tapping a rolling pin against his palm, is prepared for trouble, but Ann breaks down as she tells him of the death of her son. Her debasement is complete, but Carver rescues her from the isolated defeat in which so many of his previous protagonists have been immured. The baker apologizes, and in that instant's compassion is moved to confess his misgivings and his loneliness, and the cold remove he has kept to: "I'm not an evil man, I don't think. Not evil, like you said on the phone. You got to understand what it comes down to is I don't know how to act anymore, it would seem" (88). Their shared bond is inadequacy in the face of loss, joined by a need to be forgiven for that inadequacy. Consequently, whereas in previous stories people clutched themselves in isolated corners against their respective devastations, here they manage to come together in the communal ceremony of eating warm rolls and drinking coffee: "You have to eat and keep going. Eating is a small, good thing in a time like this" (88).

The availability of nourishment discloses their common "hunger." Ann, Howard, and the baker begin a quiet convalescence, eating what they can, talking until morning. Unlike "The Bath," whose focus is the title's solitary baptism, a purgative reflex meant to ward off catastrophe, "A Small, Good Thing" affirms the consolations of mutual acceptance. Ann and Howard had refused food throughout the story, which suggested their desperate denial. The closing scene "exteriorizes" their misery so as to make available to them the healing impulses of the baker and the small, but significant, brand of grace that human sympathy can provide.

In "Where I'm Calling From," too, commiseration instigates recuperation. In a drying-out facility where the inhabitants are identified and exiled by alcoholism, the narrator is at first unwilling or unable to relate his own story. Everyone at the facility is seized by the same trembling; everyone gauges his relative distance from everyone else's latest stage of collapse, trying to navigate through the mirrorings of his own disease.

Instead of confessing, the narrator persuades a fellow drunk, J. P., to tell his story. By recalling how conditions decayed, J. P. demonstrates a "talking cure" for impacted personalities. Whereas ritualized blandishments about willpower and self-esteem are barely sustaining to people who best recognize themselves in defeat, J. P.'s tale of how he met and married Roxy, a chimney sweep, increases the man's vigor as it frees his voice. It also clears a path for the narrator to follow out of his own eviscerated grimness.

J. P. characterizes Roxy as arrestingly natural and unselfconscious; their courtship started when J. P. was at a friend's house where she had just finished cleaning the chimney. Upon receiving payment, Roxy offered the friend a kiss for good luck, at which point J. P. decided to request the same gift. As J. P. proceeds with his story, Roxy is revealed to be neither maudlin nor promiscuous, just resilient—someone whose capacity for love derives from substantial resources of self-respect. Certainly their relationship had been the best thing to come along in J. P.'s life, until the booze preempted everything.

But Carver does not let "Where I'm Calling From" wither at this familiar impasse. Roxy arrives at the facility to visit J. P., for whom her embrace is an immediate tonic. The narrator marvels at her strength and self-assurance, which sharply contrasts with all the lurking, stalking, and shame that he has been witnessing every day: "Her hands are broad and the fingers have these big knuckles. This is a woman who can make fists if she has to" (142–143). He asks for a kiss, and she gives it easily, taking him by the shoulders as if to brace him for the treatment.

When he was twelve years old, J. P. tells the narrator, he fell down a dry well, and "everything about his life was different for him at the bottom of the well. But nothing fell on him and nothing closed off that little circle of blue. Then his dad came along with the rope, and it wasn't long before J. P. was back in the world he'd always lived in" (130). Salvation is possible, but it requires patience—the one-day-at-a-time creed of the recovering alcoholic—and the belief that "that little circle of blue" is as substantial and reliable as one's entrapment. "Where I'm Calling From" concludes with the narrator's memories of tranquility and his ultimate resolve. Whereas in "The Compartment," Myers lamented his having no idea what he might say to his son, here the narrator figures that saying "It's me" on the telephone is a way to begin again. Obviously he is in the early stage of therapy, but as he determines how to talk to his wife without argument or sarcasm and how to reconnect with his girlfriend again, it appears that where he is calling from need not diminish nor disqualify the fact that, finally, he *is calling*.

In like fashion the protagonist of "Fever" finds his anxieties mitigated by the basic inducements of human contact. One of the practical crises Carlyle must face in trying to deal with his abandonment by his wife, Eileen, for his colleague—a mutual friend and fellow high school art teacher "who'd apparently turned his grades in on time" (158)—is locating a dependable babysitter now that fall classes have begun again. His hurried choices, which include a careless teen-ager and a gruff, ghoulish woman with hairy arms, are disappointing and encourage his fear that Eileen's leaving has left unpluggable cracks everywhere.

Eileen telephones to solicit his understanding in "this matter" (recalling the plastic connotations of Inez's marital "assessment" in "Careful") and to verify her happiness, as though it might be of some indefinable consolation to him. Her unctuous earnestness exasperates him, especially because it is conveyed by the jargon of pop psychology: they are still "bonded," she is "going for it," they need to keep the "lines of communication open," he needs to adopt a "positive mental attitude," . . . and say, how's your karma? But despite what Carlyle deems her "insanity," Eileen is prescient enough to have realized that he needs a sitter for the children and a housekeeper. She provides the name of Mrs. Webster, an older woman who had once worked for Eileen's lover's mother (how civil! how sophisticated they are!) and whom she promises he can count on (in contrast, presumably, to her own inconstancy).

Whatever his doubts toward Eileen, Carlyle discovers in Mrs. Webster the kind of quiet dignity and supportiveness, particularly in her intimacies with her husband, that Holly had dreamed of in "Gazebo" as being the special province of the elderly, and indeed, that Carlyle had hoped would represent his future with Eileen. As a result of Mrs. Webster's taking over the household, Carlyle is suffused with calm; he becomes more intrepid in his relationship with his girlfriend (whom he had previously admired for her ability to equate understanding him with not pressuring him), and the family begins to thrive to the extent that Carlyle can face the truth about his wife's permanent decision not to return. When he falls ill, Mrs. Webster easily expands her ministrations to incorporate him as well as his children, and not even fever can deter his prospects for renewal, which have been due in large measure to Mrs. Webster's indiscriminate love.

When Mrs. Webster arrives one day with the news that she and her husband are leaving for Oregon to work on a mink ranch, Carlyle's initial response is panic; to be sure, the sudden shattering of one's delicate composure is common enough throughout Carver's stories, and it would not be surprising for "Fever" to conclude with Carlyle dangling over the pit of his own disarray. Eileen calls again. She has intuited her husband's distress, for which she prescribes journal writing in order to translate and extinguish his problems. But once again Carlyle figures that her craziness contaminates the communication she extols.

Nevertheless, Carlyle is spared a final breakdown. He relates the history of his relationship with Eileen to the eternally patient Mrs. Webster, who bestows her acceptance and predicts his restoration: " 'Good. Good for you,' Mrs. Webster said when she saw he had finished. 'You're made out of good stuff. And so is she—so is Mrs. Carlyle. And don't you forget it. You're both going to be okay after this is over' " (185). Consequently, Carlyle learns that he is ready to come to terms with life in the wake of loss. In fact, "loss" is a misnomer for the abiding legacy of his past, in that it "would become a part of him now, too, as surely as anything else he'd left behind" (186). Subdued, yet resolute, Carlyle turns away from the departing Websters and toward his children. This closing gesture implies his emergence from fever and vulnerability, if only to the degree that he is able to offer himself, which is the surest sign of health Carver ever provides.

"There are a few absolutes in this life, some verities, if you will," writes the author, "and we would do well not to forget them."[14] Beyond the slow wash of hopelessness throughout Carver's fiction, the stiff coil of the common run that blocks all aspiration, are those moments of fortitude and affirmation that surface in *Cathedral* and provide some positive, even sentimental, texturing that counters the savage attenuation of character, description, and outlook. Carver specifically heralds the volume's title story on these grounds: "When I Wrote 'Cathedral' I experienced this rush and I felt, 'This is what it's all about, this is the reason we do this.' "[15]

The story opens with the narrator explaining his consternation at learning that, following the death of his wife, a blind man is coming to stay at his home. His resistance to the idea is partly due to the awkwardness he anticipates—he has never known a blind person, and "in the movies, the blind moved slowly and never laughed" (209)—and partly due to the fact that the man, an old friend of the narrator's wife and with whom she has conducted a longstanding relationship of mailed tape recordings, represents a part of his wife's life that excludes him. She had been a reader for the blind man during the time of her relationship with her childhood sweetheart, a United States Air Force officer-in-training, which ended in his departure and her bungled suicide attempt. Both her lover and Robert, the blind man, were incorporated into poems that her husband cannot appreciate. Now the narrator is reluctant to endure the intrusion of a man who represents a competitive part of his own wife's life—a man who "took liberties" with her by reading her face with his hands! The awakening of his own selfishness makes the narrator sullen. He tries in vain to imagine how Robert's wife could have stood living with a man who could never see her, and in doing so exposes his own rather repellant insularity and lack of compassion.

However, Robert turns out to be a natural-born con-founder of stereotypes. He is a robust, broad-gestured man who easily gets his bearings in new surroundings: he ravages his dinner, readily accepts his host's offer to smoke some pot, and even proves quite comfortable "watching" television. The combined influence of these activities inspires unaccustomed ease in the narrator; when his wife's robe falls open after she falls asleep, he cavalierly reasons that the blind man is unaware, of course, and does not bother to cover her up again.

As the two men turn their attention to a television documentary about cathedrals, the narrator tries to ap-proximate what they are like for the sake of his guest, but "It just isn't in me to do it. I can't do any more than I've done. . . . The truth is, cathedrals don't mean any-thing special to me. Nothing. Cathedrals. They're something to look at on late-night TV" (226). At Rob-ert's suggestion the narrator gets pen and paper and together, and with Robert's hand riding on top of the narrator's, they begin drawing a cathedral. In this way the amenities of keeping company evolve into a com-munal ceremony comparable to that which closes "A Small, Good Thing." With Robert's encouragement—"Never thought anything like this could happen in your lifetime, did you, bub? Well, it's a strange life, we all know that. Go on now. Keep it up" (227)—the narrator is able to let go of his inhibitions and collaborate in an expressive vision. "It was like nothing else in my life up to now," he confesses to himself (228).

Eyes closed now, the narrator surrenders himself to Robert's gentle guidance, much as Carlyle gave himself over to Mrs. Webster's care in "Fever." Both stories, along with "A Small, Good Thing" and "Where I'm Calling From," emphasize the abundant compensations of shared experience. The protagonists of these stories are not necessarily more articulate than their precursors—the narrator of "Cathedral" can only come up with " 'It's really something' " to appreciate the spiritual climax of the story—but they are available to depths of feeling they need not name to justify. If the images that conclude the richest stories in *Cathedral* are gestures by heavy hands—the breaking of bread against suffering or the unblinding of the blind—they begin to establish a basis for conduct beyond the limits set by stylistic austerity or introversion clung to like some ethical stance. A blind man whose wife has died and a man who admits that he does not believe in anything join together to create a cathedral. It is neither perfect nor complete, but the process is encouraging and adequate for now. Robert's belief in the concluding story is known throughout the volume: it *is* a strange life. The most sympathetic, most human of Carver's characters "keep it up" anyway.

Notes

1. Quoted in William L. Stull, "Raymond Carver," *Dictionary of Literary Biography: 1984*, ed. Jean W. Ross (Detroit: Gale, 1985) 242.

CATHEDRAL

2. Carver notes that the stories in *Cathedral* reflect what has been the most "composed" period of his life: "I feel more comfortable with myself, able to give more. Maybe it's getting older and getting smarter. I don't know. Or getting older and more stupid. But I feel closer to this book than to anything I've ever done." Ray Anello and Rebecca Boren, interview, *Time* 5 Sept. 1983: 67.

3. Raymond Carver, "Feathers," *Cathedral* (New York: Knopf, 1983) 25. Further references to stories in this collection are noted parenthetically in the text.

4. Michael J. Bugeja views this as a crucial structural flaw in the story. See "Tarnish and Silver: An Analysis of Carver's *Cathedral,*" *South Dakota Review* 24 (1986): 77–80.

5. Citing this story, Michael Gorra complains that Carver's style actually "dictates rather then embodies his characters' predicament" ("Laughter and Bloodshed," *Hudson Review* 37 [1984]: 156). A similar dissent is registered by T. Coraghessan Boyle against the formulaic tedium of the "Catatonic Realists": "You know the story, you've read it a thousand times: Three characters are sitting around the kitchen of a trailer, saying folksy things to one another. Finally one of them gets up to go to the bathroom and the author steps in to end it with a line like, 'It was all feathers' " ("A Symposium on Contemporary American Fiction," *Michigan Quarterly Review* 26 [1987]: 707).

6. John Cheever, "The Five-Forty-Eight," *The Housebreaker of Shady Hill and Other Stories* (New York: Harper, 1958). "The Five-Forty-Eight" earned the Benjamin Franklin Short Story Award in 1955.

7. Cheever, 134.

8. Mark A. R. Facknitz, "Missing the Train: Raymond Carver's Sequel to John Cheever's 'The Five-Forty-Eight,' " *Studies in Short Fiction* 22 (1985): 347.

9. Marc Chenetier, "Living On/Off the 'Reserve': Performance, Interrogation, and Negativity in the Works of Raymond Carver," *Critical Angles: European Views of Contemporary American Literature*, ed. Marc Chenetier (Carbondale: Southern Illinois University Press, 1986) 173. Chenetier maintains that Carver's method "bludgeons presence upon the reader" through his "violent economy"; however, "past the opening lines the text proceeds to unravel into misdirection" (166).

10. Quoted in Larry McCaffery and Sinda Gregory, "An Interview with Raymond Carver" *Mississippi Review* 40/41 (Winter 1985); 66.

11. "The Bath," *What We Talk About When We Talk About Love* (New York: Knopf, 1981) 54.

12. William L. Stull, "Beyond Hopelessville: Another Side of Raymond Carver," *Philological Quarterly* 64 (1985): 7–9.

13. Stull, "Beyond Hopelessville" 10.

14. Quoted in Stull, "Raymond Carver" 242.

15. Quoted in Mona Simpson, interview, "The Art of Fiction LXXVI," *Paris Review* 25 (1983): 207.

CHAPTER SIX

Poetry

Although Raymond Carver reports that he has made "the right choice" in focusing his talents on the writing of fiction, he has maintained a steady "secondary" output of poetry throughout his career.[1] Certainly, poems are particularly compatible with Carver's self-proclaimed devotion to short forms and small presses. In general, under the greater restriction that these most "minimal" of verbal spaces demand, his poems at times read more like object lessons than do their fictional counterparts, vaunting their ironies and protests like formulas. The disquieting lurches that have become trademarks of the stories give way to relatively composed—both meditative and completed—reactions in the poems.

In an afterword to the *Fires* collection, Carver discloses his motives for reordering the original chronology of publication, noting his preference for a more subjective arrangement based upon "a constellation of feelings and attitudes" or "obsessions" that, in retrospect, dominate his early work (roughly speaking, those poems written between 1966 and 1982).[2] The prevailing topic of the first group is alcohol. Drinking is perhaps the predominant crutch and complaint in the fiction, mirroring its prominence in the author's personal life. Nevertheless, even though the treatment of this theme in the poetry is more explicit than in stories like "Mr. Coffee and Mr. Fixit" or "One More Thing" (where it lies insistently in the background), Carver still resists speculative extravagance. As in the fiction the narrative quality of the poems is edgy, oblique. Lyricism is muted at every turn, engendering a poetry of instants that often as not leaves the speaker gaping.

Any minute now, something will happen.
  —"Drinking While Driving"

you wonder how long this can go on.
  —"Your Dog Dies"

      Father, I love you,
yet how can I say thank you, I who can't hold my liquor
  either, and don't even know the places to fish?
  —"Photograph of My Father in His Twenty-Second Year"

I hope someday to forget all this.
  —"Iowa Summer"

Part of the trauma of alcoholism is its disintegrating effects not only upon social and familial obligations but upon the artistic transaction as well. Occasionally, as in "Cheers," the trials of hangovers or of shaky abstinence are alleviated by a sardonicism that masquerades as vigor. But the old indictment of the minimalists—they "speak softly and carry no stick whatsoever"[3]—is especially formidable here.

What Carver does uphold even in this opening section is the value, if not the authoritativeness, of the little guy, whose intentions are more stalwart than his prowess:

"That anonymous husband, barefooted,
humiliated, trying to save his life, he
is the hero of this poem."
—"The Baker"

"All poems are love poems," one learns in "For Semra, With Martial Vigor," and when the recipients of those poems are brought low by their own weaknesses and admissions, the love Carver bestows is simple and poignant.

The long poem "You Don't Know What Love Is" constitutes the second section of *Fires*. It transcribes a half-invented, venomous disquisition on antisentimentalism by the cantankerous Charles Bukowski. (Carver's Bukowski is only slightly more outrageous than the self-promoting cult author himself.) Even if all poems are love poems, the comprehensive nature of love is often scurrilous or perverse. The speaker derides his reverent college audience for their reductive, sanitized expectations, proclaiming that one must earn the right either to talk about love (recalling Mel's frustration over definitions in "What We Talk About When We Talk About Love") or to hope to understand it:

What do any of you know about life
What do any of you know about anything
Which of you here has been fired from a job
or else has beaten up your broad
or else has been beaten up by your broad (60).

For such a poet, love lines are a bloodletting, a down-and-dirty affair of the heart, groin, and spleen. Surprisingly, Carver's Bukowski and his Balzac ("Balzac") meet on this issue: both are earthy men who will not tolerate the proprieties that threaten to inhibit artistic license.

When Carver turns to "foreign travel and personages," it is to resume the identical obsessions of the other poems, thereby granting them a sort of universality. "Morning, Thinking of Empire," for example, depicts the failure of an exotic backdrop to overcome the familiar interplay of love and ruin; "Surely we have diminished one another" is the thought that obstructs the scenery (65). A consideration of Flaubert's world of desire leads the poet to masturbation and a demystifying confrontation with the "fiery leaning into consequence" that is at the root of all passion ("The Blue Stones" 6). At "The Mosque in Jaffa," in the midst of treachery,

The key words fly out—
Turks Greeks Arabs Jews
trade worship love murder
a beautiful woman.
He grins again at such foolishness (72).

Thus, with his insufficiencies given international verification, the poet grows no more confident about his in-

terpretive faculties for all his travels. The overall sense
of this section is one of fidgety attentiveness; the poet's
alienation is intensified by his general lassitude and his
belatedness:

Must I ever remain behind—
listening, smoking,
scribbling down the next far thing?
—"This Room" 77

"Things domestic and familiar" feature rhapsodic
appreciations of the outdoors. Although the virtues of
evacuation—getting out into nature and out of oneself—
have been abandoned to some degree as a subject since
Furious Seasons, these virtues retain their hold over the
entirety of Carver's poetic output. The composure that
is absent in so many of the fictionalized marital relationships arises in the unspoken community of salmon fishermen in "Near Klamath," who enjoy the rewards of
shared appetites and physical satisfactions; they move
upstream with ritualistic forbearance, "slowly, full of
love, toward the still pools" (83). Hunting, fishing, and
logging are championed as accesses to secret compacts
with the natural world, the source of wholesome attitudes. Desperation is diagnosed as the plague of world-
liness and often precipitates a prayer for radical
dispossession.

The mind would like to get out of here
onto the snow. It would like to run
with a pack of shaggy animals, all teeth,
under the moon, across the snow, leaving

no prints, or spoor, nothing behind.
—"Winter Insomnia" 85

Carver locates these poems between the disparate realms of coursing fish and tract homes, between the dreamy seclusion of dark fields and delicate streams and the shrill neon landscape of cable television, fast food, and private corruption. The eccentricities and arcana of outdoorsmen provide assurances and exits that it would be sacrilege to let language intrude too heavily upon:

But my dad was right. I mean
he kept silent and looked into the river,
worked his tongue, like a thought, behind the bait.
—"Bobber" 98

In "Highway 99E from Chico" (99), the "chuckle" of sleeping ducks, the slump of the tules beneath the weight of blackbirds, and the intimate clinging of wet leaves to the poet's windshield occasion a shudder of joy that needs only be confessed, never analyzed or excused. When the poet does try to do more, to explicate the sensation, as in "The Cougar" (100), he realizes the futility of stalking so lordly an animal across the page.

Opposing the welcome captivity of the poet to pure images are the brute facts of personal distress. Not even the brilliant, numbing isolation of "Deschutes River" staves off the gnawing awareness that "Far away—/ another man is raising my children, bedding my wife bedding my wife" (108). Perhaps the poet's withdrawal denies him even the right to indignation; certainly it makes the sight of a cruelly proficient badger tearing its rabbit bluntly symbolic. The point is that present contentment cannot be ensured without an articulate, composed past. Refuting those privileged moments of relief is the stunning reproach of a wife's "weeping and writing in our new kitchen" ("The Other Life" 94). When a bereaved son asks, by way of valediction, "After tonight / how can I ever go back to that / other life?" ("Forever" 109), he seeks to assuage his grief over his father's death with the vain hope that his future might be extricated from these memories, this town. And in "The Mailman as Cancer Patient," a dying man despises his nostalgic dreams.

for when he wakes
there's nothing left; it is
as if he'd never been
anywhere, never done anything;
there is just the room,
the early morning without sun,
the sound of a doorknob
turning slowly (95).

In each instance, personal resources and reference points have been spoiled or mislaid. The form of the poems is sketchy, cautious; the distrust of too many words, which caused the speaker to yield before the preemptive wonder of the natural world, leads him to adopt this stilted technique and to assume that the only real resolution he can reach is the belief that one must be hard-boiled in the face of old and enduring injuries.[4]

So Carver's people drift helplessly, awaiting "the next cruel turn of circumstance, and then the next" ("Marriage" 92).

"Indigence is at the root of our lives, yes / but this is not right" ("Movement" 8), the poet announces in *Where Water Comes Together with Other Water* (1985). As ever, sex, alcohol, violence, and self-pity cause the principal damage, as well as constitute the habitual response to it:

Would I live my life over again?
Make the same unforgivable mistakes?
Yes, given half a chance. Yes.
—"Rain" 38

Chronic suffering drains even the energy required for despair, leaving only a tired cynicism, a listless voice disgusted with its own complaint and its perpetual tally of losses:

We wanted to get down on our knees
and say forgive us our sins, forgive us
our lives. But it was too late.
Too late. No one around would listen.
—"Anathema" 30

The situation bears no discussion, for language remains an imperfect and terribly expensive instrument:

He narrows his eyes against the smoke. From time
to time he uses the ashtray as he waits
for her to finish weeping.
—"The Ashtray" 15

POETRY

Bursting the spirit's sleep are poems about the abiding comforts of nature. The forest of "Elk Camp," redolent with firs and imaginings (87), the satisfactions glimpsed in "an older, fiercer order of things" in "Eagles" (120), or the love of rivers "that increases me" ("Where Water Comes Together with Other Water" 17) are charged with pleasure; poems like "My Boat" and "My Crow" take a delight in distilling life's best, cleanest images that is absolutely greedy. The word "happiness" in this collection comes as an elemental surprise, like a shock of cold river water.

Carver's poems seemed designed to honor the landscape, not to dominate it with soaring language. The poet does not wish to disturb the poised moment, nor does he venture to compete with the remarkable, as memorably shown in "My Dad's Wallet," in which the corpse of the speaker's father, "restless / even in death" (55), is transported to the family plot. Faced with the mundane concerns of payment—grotesque, stupid intrusions into the family grief—the undertaker, the widow, and her son stare at the dead man's wallet:

Nobody said anything.
All the life had gone out of that wallet.
It was old and rent and soiled.
But it was my dad's wallet. And she opened
it and looked inside. Drew out
a handful of money that would go
toward this last, most astounding, trip (56).

This is poetry that takes notice but stands clear. "A man

has to begin over and over—to try to think and feel only in a very limited field," advises Sherwood Anderson in the epigraph to "Harley's Swans" (83). The poems imply that reform is under way, but they do not engineer that reform. A cleansing of the mind, a hand raised on behalf of decency—these substitute for linguistic resonance and intrepidness. At best, modesty promotes precision; Carver gives way to the world.

Ultramarine (1986) reflects the greater generosity of spirit that has been heralded by some of the stories in *Cathedral*. The poet continues to contend with Death's insidious approach and with domestic trials, either of which can transform life into "a stone, grinding and sharpening" ("The Autopsy Room" 16) or overwhelm artistic faculties altogether: "Nothing adds up. / It all adds up. How long will this storm go on?" ("Stupid" 22). However, after long negotiation with his ghosts, he seems better able to strike a balance between escape and duty, as exemplified by the concluding lines of "This Morning":

But for a minute or two I did forget
myself and everything else. I know I did.
For when I turned back I didn't know
where I was. Until some birds rose up
from the gnarled trees. And flew
in the direction I needed to be going (4).

A provisional ease has been won which makes relationships a bit less consternating and tempers memories of

POETRY

family misunderstandings, burned-out passions, or alcoholic wreckage with opportunities for renewal:

There isn't enough of anything
as long as we live. But at intervals
a sweetness appears and, given a chance,
prevails.
—"The Author of Her Misfortune" 51

The chief compensations are simple, natural: the abundant, lunging waters of the Pacific Northwest or the redemptive powers of human compassion. Solace is as inexplicable as strife, but *Ultramarine* celebrates the legitimacy of sensations that finally need no additional comment. If it is true that, as one reviewer writes, "sanity best displays itself as gratitude,"[5] perhaps wisdom best displays itself as peace of mind:

We're extraordinarily calm and tender with each other
as if sensing the other's rickety state of mind.
As if we knew what the other was feeling. We don't,
of course. We never do. No matter.
It's the tenderness I care about.
—"The Gift" 140

A peace that surpasses understanding is all the more precious for being beyond the poet's clever manufacture, and will suffice.

UNDERSTANDING RAYMOND CARVER

Notes

1. Carver offers this personal assessment in his interview with Mona Simpson, "The Art of Fiction LXXVI," *Paris Review* 25 (1983): 216. He goes on to explain that the revised poems that constitute the poetry selection in *Fires* represent what he deems the most worthy examples from the three early collections *Near Klamath* (1968), *Winter Insomnia* (1970), and *At Night the Salmon Move* (1976). Accordingly, in commenting on Carver's poetry, I have focused on *Fires: Essays, Poems, Stories* (Santa Barbara: Capra, 1983) and on two recent collections, *Where Water Comes Together with Other Water* (Random, 1985) and *Ultramarine* (Random, 1986); all page references are to these volumes and are noted parenthetically in the text.

2. *Fires* 217

3. Rosellen Brown, "The Emperor's New Fiction," *Boston Review* Aug. 1986: 8.

4. Some critics of the poetry contend that this technique, effective as it is in the fiction, hobbles the poetry. For example, Carol Muske complains that Carver relies on "a loose, talky stanza built on the model of his prose paragraph" that makes the poems read rather like "rehearsals for poems, anecdotes precedent to poetry" ("Disk Jockeys, Eggplants and Desparecidos," *New York Times Book Review* 9 Feb. 1986: 28). Likewise, in his review in *Poetry* (Oct. 1985), Dave Smith fears that Carver "can be terribly maudlin, sentimental, clunky. As poet, perhaps, Carver is a kind of primitive painter, an acquired taste" (40). Thus, despite his general appreciation of the poems, Smith also implies that Carver's method may be too relentless, too internally disrupted, to achieve consistently successful poetry.

5. Patricia Hempl, "Surviving a Life in the Present," *New York Times Book Review* 7 June 1987: 15.

CONCLUSION

While critics may cheer the stemming, if not the reversal, of the corruptive descent of the Carver hero in *Cathedral*, the daily crush remains more memorable than the cure. Subsequent stories retain the transitional character of that collection. There are dissenting voices against eclipse, but they are faint. At present, vital signs are relatively stable, but the situation remains critical.

Actually, two recently published stories seem rather reactionary—restored to the orbit and attitude of Carver's earlier collections. "Whoever Was Using This Bed" revisits the theme of feverish sleeplessness that proved so durable in *Will You Please Be Quiet, Please?* and *What We Talk About When We Talk About Love*. An important difference here may be the fact that both the husband and wife are awake and equally distressed by nightmares, mysterious wrong numbers, delayed tremors from old relationships, and fears of catastrophic illness. Still, the conversation that carries them through the raw wee hours of the morning becomes a contest of exclusionary anxieties, as though love equals accessibil-

ity to exploitation for the sake of attention and consoling. Because they drift out of their normal depth when
they discuss their troubles, they shudder to have to confront the truth about themselves:

What I've just said to her, what I've been thinking
about off and on all day, well, I feel as if I've crossed
some kind of invisible line. I feel as if I've come to a
place I never thought I'd have to come to. And I don't
know how I got here. It's a strange place. It's a place
where a little harmless dreaming and then some
sleepy, early-morning talk has led me into
considerations of death and annihilation.[1]

In "Blackbird Pie," too, there appears to be nothing particularly redemptive about knowledge.[2] The narrator
has an extraordinary memory. His mind is a rich stew of
historical battles and treaties, yet the many names and
dates merely upholster his solitude. A letter from his
wife detailing her grievances and ending with ultima-
tums seems to him absolutely foreign; the very hand-
writing strikes him as unrecognizable.[3] Like the couple
in "Whoever Was Using This Bed" and the majority of
previous Carver protagonists, he can only tolerate the
most provisional of confrontations.

On the other hand, "Boxes" and "Elephant" give
grounds for greater optimism. "Boxes" borrows an image from "Preservation"—eating defrosted food to stave
off decay and waste—but manages to revise the sober-

ing implications of that story.[4] The narrator's elderly mother, having left California for Longview despite her son's discouragement, has ended up hating the place and is preparing to return to California, as though her happiness had somehow been mislaid there. The narrator realizes that he may never see her again, and rightly reasons that this latest migration of hers will bring her no peace. He understands that despite her having been a perpetual chide, she is an integral part of him, and his relief at her going is moderated by remorse. When she calls from California to complain about the heavy traffic, the worsening pollen, the oppressive weather, and her disreputable building manager, he discovers in himself a genuine affection for her; he calls her "dear," the way he remembers his father used to do, and tells her not to be afraid. He witnesses a brief embrace outside his window and wonders about the affectionate reflexes that are so taken for granted and are yet so consequential—a word of forgiveness, a token of hope.

Then there is the narrator of "Elephant," who is working himself to exhaustion to keep his mother, brother, ex-wife, and children financially afloat. Their litany of hardships makes him panicky and resentful. He dreams of taking vengeance upon his own family; he threatens to move to Australia to avoid their ever-increasing demands. But he has another dream, in which he is a child again riding on his father's broad, sustaining shoulders. When he awakens he understands that he is not going to run away after all, of course, and with acceptance comes an unaccountable feeling of optimism that arrives like a shock of grace. "But things were bound to change soon. Things would pick up in the fall maybe. There was lots to hope for."[5] He takes a walk, increases his pace, even begins to whistle. He verifies his love for his debtors, and for once he feels charity for them when always before there had only been money to give them to keep them off. The story concludes with his catching a ride with a friend in his big car, which has not yet been paid off. But, so what? They zoom off, and the moment is glorious and intoxicating.

As poet Mark Strand puts it in "Keeping Things Whole," "We all have reasons / for moving. / I move / to keep things whole."[6] Still, compared to the sound of bottoms dropping out everywhere in Carver's fiction, reports of "lots to hope for" may be a bit too shrill to be persuasive and too insubstantial to last. The paralytic conditions of minimalist fiction militate against bolder examples of optimism. Although Carver's stories inspire speculation, they themselves refuse to speculate; they at once develop and indict the expressive resources of language.

Ultimately, the prospects for the vindication of Carver's characters must remain a function of their verbal abilities; interpersonal relationships can only proceed so far as their language dictates. "Language most shews a man," wrote Ben Jonson. "Speak that I may see thee." Identity is not simply augmented by how well people conduct themselves in words; it is comprised by words. Therefore, it may be that individual conscious-

CONCLUSION

ness is predicated upon a more substantial social foundation than minimalism ordinarily provides.

The consequences are everywhere present in Carver's stories, in which the potential for meaningful interaction is squandered whenever characters despair of "stating themselves" effectively. As Martin Buber interprets this impasse, "The mysterious intercourse between two human worlds becomes only a game" and "all reality begins to disintegrate."[7] Russian language theorist Mikhail Bakhtin corroborates this assessment of the social grounding of being: "No Nirvana is possible for a single consciousness. A single consciousness is a contradiction in terms. Consciousness is essentially multiple."[8] The failure of abiding mutuality between husband and wife, parent and child, or friend and friend is conspicuous throughout the minimalist landscape, no less than is the terseness of structure and tone; the deadly alignments of familiar environments and constricting relationships find their counterparts in dull ruts of speech. Spans of attention are curtailed, selves amputated. Social intercourse diminishes into a series of empty scrimmages.

Were Carver diagnosing contemporary ills from the command post of verbal superiority over his "minimized" subjects, the evolution of his attitude might be justified stylistically. But the same silences that rob his characters of contacts constrain the author to monosyllabic probings—hardly conducive to the manufacture of optimistic resolution, much less to deliverance from the general malaise. No wonder that the hope that concludes more recent stories like "Boxes" and "Elephant" must be vague, modest, or even hackneyed.

The prerequisites for breakthrough have not altered. First among them is a fullness of expression to accommodate the fulfillment of desire. "A single piano cannot be used to play" the symphonic complexities of swollen consciousness and psychological dynamism. "The answer to how such scope can be achieved through the techniques of minimalism," declares one dissenting writer, "is that it can't."[9] Bereft of the capacity for generating more than thin strings of simple subjects and verbs, neither reduced literary characters nor their reductive authors are likely to escape confinement.

In the absence of amplitude or intellectual surge, Carver gets sentimental when he tries to play a few hunches against the consensus of desensitization. Here, then, is the great pitfall of "achieved" minimalism: at zero degrees, everything registers equally, from brand names to brave resolve. To borrow a title from Ann Beattie, "falling in place" is more convincing than the soul's progress.[10] With events and artistic practices so boxed in as they are, Carver's homely stories only allow so much room to *believe* in.

"We're nice people, all of us, to a point," declares a chronic adulterer in "Menudo," and, indeed, before long, the old pantomime of commitment dissolves into "compulsion and error."[11] Nevertheless, decency is possible; perseverance is possible. In the end, heroism for Carver is not cunning but compassion. A man offers a kind word, remembers to hug his wife as he leaves for

CONCLUSION

work, promises to be home in time for dinner—these are responsive, responsible acts that merit regard. "True, in the grander scheme of things, his return will be an event of small moment—but an event nonetheless."[12]

Carver's is a tough world to love. All manner of trauma threatens to close people off: alcoholism, unemployment, betrayal, anxiety, despondency. A refusal to knuckle under becomes a mark of distinction when the ground rules are that everyone is a target, and life is survival of the resilient. Carver defines health as a propensity for reintegration, but the going is cautious, a matter of stammered complaints and minimal gains. As he strives for fuller forms of expression, Carver seldom casts a wider net, but he does seem increasingly willing to qualify the nature of captivity. He maintains that his goal has always been to recognize the essential nobility of "people doing the best they could." Modest achievements can turn out to be the small, good things that ready the desolate for recovery and that entitle the reader to be "reminded of his humanness." "I know I make more of it than I should, but I think it's a noble undertaking, this business," says the author in defense of his art. "It beats a lot of other things I can think of."[13]

Notes

1. "Whoever Was Using This Bed," *New Yorker* 28 Apr. 1986: 40.

2. "Blackbird Pie," *New Yorker* 7 July 1986: 26–34.

3. A similar nonresponse is depicted in "Intimacy," *Esquire* Aug. 1986: 58–60, when a man visits his resentful former wife: "As soon as I sit down she brings me some coffee. Then she comes out with what's on her mind. She says I've caused her anguish, made her feel exposed and humiliated. Make no mistake, I feel I'm home" (58). Her tirade elicits his mute, abject supplication, but he can manage only the vaguest sense that "somebody ought to make an effort here" to improve conditions (60).

4. "Boxes," *New Yorker* 24 Feb. 1986: 31–37.

5. "Elephant," *New Yorker* 9 June 1986:45.

6. Mark Strand, "Keeping Things Whole," *Reasons for Moving* (New York: Atheneum, 1975) 40.

7. Martin Buber, "Between Man and Man: The Realms," *The Human Dialogue: Perspectives in Communication*, ed. Floyd W. Watson and Ashley Montague (New York: Macmillan, 1967) 117.

8. Quoted in Caryl Emerson, "The Outer World and Inner Speech: Bakhtin, Vygotsky, and Internalization of Language," *Critical Inquiry* 10 (1983): 257. For further development of the nature of the separation of Self from Other in contemporary fiction, see my essay "Communication and Resistance: On Opaque Fictions," *Publications of the Missouri Philological Association* 11 (1986): 53–60.

9. Linsey Abrams, "A Maximalist Novelist Looks at Some Minimalist Fiction," *Mississippi Review* 40/41 (Winter 1985): 30.

10. Ann Beattie, *Falling in Place* (New York: Random, 1980).

11. "Menudo," *Granta* 21 (1987): 159, 163.

12. "Menudo," 171.

13. Quoted in Bruce Weber, "Raymond Carver: A Chronicler of Blue-Collar Despair," *New York Times Magazine* 24 June 1984: 50.

BIBLIOGRAPHY

Works by Raymond Carver
Fiction
Put Yourself in My Shoes. Santa Barbara, CA: Capra, 1974.
Will You Please Be Quiet, Please? New York: McGraw-Hill, 1976.
Furious Seasons and Other Stories. Santa Barbara, CA: Capra, 1977.
What We Talk About When We Talk About Love. New York: Knopf, 1981; London: Collins, 1982.
The Pheasant. Worcester, MA: Metacom, 1982.
Cathedral. New York: Knopf, 1983; London: Collins, 1984.
The Stories of Raymond Carver. London: Picador, 1985.
Poetry
Near Klamath. Sacramento: English Club of Sacramento State College, 1968.
Winter Insomnia. Santa Cruz, CA: Kayak, 1970.
At Night the Salmon Move. Santa Barbara, CA: Capra, 1976.
Two Poems. Salisbury, MD: Scarab, 1982.
If It Please You. Northridge, CA: Lord John, 1984.
This Water. Concord, NH: Ewert, 1985.
Where Water Comes Together with Other Water. New York: Random, 1985.
Ultramarine. New York: Random, 1986.
Collection
Fires: Essays, Poems, Stories. Santa Barbara, CA: Capra, 1983; London: Collins, 1985. Includes the essays "On Writing" and "Fires," and the stories "Distance," "The Lie," "The Cabin," "Harry's Death," "The Pheasant," "Where Is Everyone?" and "So Much Water so Close to Home."
Selected Uncollected Fiction in Periodicals
"The Aficionados." *Toyon* 9 (1963): 5–9. (Appears under the pen name John Vale.)
"The Hair." *Toyon* 9 (1963): 27–30.

BIBLIOGRAPHY

"Poseidon and Company." *Toyon* 9 (1963): 24–25.

"Bright Red Apples." *Gato Magazine* 2 (1967): 8–13.

"from The Augustine Notebooks." *Iowa Review* 10 (1979): 38–42.

"Boxes." *New Yorker* 24 Feb. 1986: 31–37.

"Whoever Was Using This Bed." *New Yorker* 28 Apr. 1986: 33–40.

"Elephant." *New Yorker* 9 June 1986: 38–45.

"Blackbird Pie." *New Yorker* 7 July 1986: 26–34.

"Intimacy." *Esquire* Aug. 1986: 58–60.

"Menudo." *Granta* 21 (1987): 157–72.

"Errand." *New Yorker* 1 June 1987: 30–36.

Miscellaneous Appearances

Ploughshares 9 (1983). Special fiction issue edited by Raymond Carver.

Foreword to *On Becoming a Novelist*, by John Gardner (New York: Harper, 1983).

Foreword to *We Are Not in This Together*, by William Kittredge. (Port Townsend, WA: Graywolf, 1984).

Dostoevsky: The Screenplay. Santa Barbara, CA: Capra, 1985.

A Celebration for Stanley Kunitz by Twenty-Five Poets. Riverdale-on-Hudson, NY: Sheep Meadow, 1985.

American Short Story Masterpieces ed. Raymond Carver and Tom Jenks. New York: Delacourte, 1987.

Introduction to *The Best American Short Stories, 1986*. ed. Shannon Ravenal and Raymond Carver. Boston: Houghton Mifflin, 1987.

Works about Raymond Carver
Selected Interviews

Bonetti, Kay. "Ray Carver: Keeping It Short." *Saturday Review* Sept.–Oct. 1983: 21–23.

BIBLIOGRAPHY

McCaffery, Larry and Sinda Gregory. "An Interview with Raymond Carver." *Mississippi Review* 40/41 (Winter 1985): 62–82.

McElhinny, Lisa. "Raymond Carver Speaking." *Akros Review* 8/9 (Spring 1984): 103–14.

Simpson, Mona. "The Art of Fiction LXXVI." *Paris Review* 25 (1983): 192–221.

Critical Analyses

Abrams, Linsey. "A Maximalist Novelist Looks at Some Minimalist Fiction." *Mississippi Review* 40/41 (Winter 1985): 24–30. Describes the techniques of defamiliarization used by Carver and other minimalists and how they potentially result in an inauthentic reduction of scope.

Atlas, James. "Less Is Less." *Atlantic* June 1981: 96–98. Complains (in representative fashion) that the severity of Carver's artistic method fails to satisfy the desire for a fuller, more solicitous reading experience.

Barth, John. "A Few Words about Minimalism." *New York Times Book Review* 28 Dec. 1986; 1–2, 25. Gives the defining features of the minimalist "esthetic" and proposes the social and historical realities from which it seems to derive.

Boxer, David and Cassandra Phillips. "*Will You Please Be Quiet, Please?* Voyeurism, Dissociation, and the Art of Raymond Carver." *Iowa Review* 10 (1979): 75–90. Discusses the nature and exploitation of the theme of voyeurism in Carver's first short story collection.

Bugeja, Michael. "Tarnish and Silver: An Analysis of Carver's *Cathedral*." *South Dakota Review* 24 (1986): 73–87. Maintains that despite the greater development of stories in this volume, many suffer from endings that are too pat or implausible.

Chénetier, Marc. "Living On/Off the 'Reserve': Performance, Interrogation, and Negativity in the Works of Raymond Carver." *Critical Angles: European Views of Contemporary Amer-*

ican Literature. Ed. Marc Chénetier. Carbondale: Southern Illinois University Press, 1986. 164–90. Contends that Carver's so-called "realism" actually works to expose the obsolescence of mimetic concepts of the use of language.

Facknitz, Mark A. R. "Missing the Train: Raymond Carver's Sequel to John Cheever's 'The Five-Forty-Eight.' " *Studies in Short Fiction* 22 (1985): 345–47. Details the nature of Carver's debt to and departure from Cheever's original story.

Gorra, Michael. "Laughter and Bloodshed." *Hudson Review* 37 (1984): 151–64. Says that the principal restraint upon Carver's characters may be the confining style he imposes upon them.

Herzinger, Kim A. "Introduction: On the New Fiction." *Mississippi Review* 40/41 (Winter 1985): 7–22. Coins the term *minimalism* and investigates ties to realism and postmodernism, as well as conjectures about the reasons behind the style's appeal.

Howe, Irving. "Stories of Our Loneliness." *New York Times Book Review* 11 Sept. 1983: 1, 42–43. Declares that *Cathedral* moves beyond the crafted tautness of the previous volumes in favor of greater ease and nuance.

LeClair, Thomas. "Fiction Chronicle—June 1981." *Contemporary Literature* 23 (1982): 83–91. Says that Carver obeys the verbal limitation of his characters so that fictional style itself becomes a metaphor for life style.

Lohafer, Susan. *Coming to Terms with the Short Story*. Baton Rouge: Louisiana State University Press, 1983. 50, 62–65ff. Shows that Carver eschews techniques of embedding that would ordinarily "thicken" narrative style.

Lonnquist, Barbara C. "Narrative Displacement and Literary Faith: Raymond Carver's inheritance from Flannery O'Connor." *Since Flannery O'Connor: Essays on the Contemporary*

BIBLIOGRAPHY

American Short Story. Ed. Loren Logsdon and Charles W. Mayer. Macomb: Western Illinois University Press, 1987. 142–50. Analyzes Carver's inheritance from O'Connor in *Cathedral* in that both authors work within, yet displace expectations of, traditional short story form.

Newman, Charles. "What's Left Out of Literature." *New York Times Book Review* 12 July 1987: 1, 24–25. Accuses Carver, Beattie, and other deliberately "flat" stylists of surrendering to enervation and "cultural weightlessness."

Smith, Allan Lloyd. "Brain Damage: The Word and the World in Postmodernist Writing." *Contemporary American Fiction*. Ed. Malcolm Bradbury and Sigmund Ro. London: Edward Arnold, 1987. 39–52. Argues that the sense of urgency in Carver's characters is reined in by their inarticulateness.

Stevenson, Diane. "Minimalist Fiction and Critical Doctrine." *Mississippi Review* 40/41 (Winter 1985): 83–89. Suggests that minimalist fiction popularizes a specifically middle-class humanism.

Stull, William L. "Beyond Hopelessville: Another Side of Raymond Carver." *Philological Quarterly* 64 (1985): 1–15. discusses how Carver's reworking of "The Bath" into "A Small, Good Thing" increases the spiritual dimension of his characters.

———. "Raymond Carver." *Dictionary of Literary Biography Yearbook: 1984*. Ed. Jean W. Ross. Detroit: Gale, 1985, 233–45. Offers a comprehensive summary of Carver's life and career, as well as a bibliography of works by and about the author.

Vander Weele, Michael. "Raymond Carver and the Language of Desire." *Denver Quarterly* 22 (1987): 108–22. Argues that even as Carver's fiction reduces contemporary social crises to imaginable size, the obstruction of meaningful discourse keeps desire unspecific and unsatisfied.

BIBLIOGRAPHY

Weber, Bruce. "Raymond Carver: A Chronicler of Blue-Collar Despair." *New York Times Magazine* 24 June 1984: 36–50. Provides a general introduction to Carver's themes and reputation and explores intersections between the author's life and his developing style.

Wilde, Alan. *Middle Grounds: Studies in Contemporary American Fiction.* Philadelphia: University of Pennsylvania Press, 1987. 110–20. Takes issue with the "catatonic realism" exemplified by Carver, Beattie, Didion, and Robison in the chapter entitled "Shooting for Smallness: Realism and Midfiction," accusing these writers of closing off potential through their restrictive assumptions about the limits of humanism.

INDEX

This index does not include references to material in the notes.

183

INDEX

INDEX

INDEX

INDEX

INDEX

Printed in the United States
95410LV00002B/57/A